Swedenborg and Esoteric Islam

SWEDENBORG STUDIES / No. 4
Monographs of the Swedenborg Foundation

Henry Corbin (1903–1978)

Swedenborg and Esoteric Islam

Henry Corbin

Translated by Leonard Fox

SWEDENBORG FOUNDATION

West Chester, Pennsylvania

First edition published 1995
Seventh printing 2022

"Mundus Imaginalis" and "Herméneutique spirituelle comparée" first appeared in Henri Corbin, *Face de Dieu, face de l'homme* (Paris: Flammarion, 1984). Reprinted by permission. Translated by Leonard Fox.

Swedenborg Studies is a scholarly series published by the Swedenborg Foundation. The primary purpose of the series is to make materials available for understanding the life and thought of Emanuel Swedenborg (1688–1772) and the impact that his thought has had on others. The Foundation undertakes to publish original studies and English translations of such studies and to republish primary sources that are otherwise difficult to access. Proposals should be sent to: Editor, Swedenborg Studies, Swedenborg Foundation, 320 North Church Street, West Chester, PA 19380.

Library of Congress Cataloging-in-Publication Data

Corbin, Henry.
[Mundus imaginalis. English]
Swedenborg and esoteric Islam : two studies / Henry Corbin : translated by Leonard Fox
p. cm. -- (Swedenborg studies : no. 4)
Translated from the French.
Contents: Mundus imaginalis -- Comparative spiritual hermeneutics
ISBN 0-87785-183-2 (paper)
1. Ishrāqīyah. 2. Imagination--Religious aspects--Islam.
3. Symbolism in the Koran. 4. Koran--Hermeneutics. 5. Shi'ah--Doctrines.
6. Swedenborg, Emanuel, 1688–1772--Contributions in biblical hermeneutics.
7. Bible--Hermeneutics. 8. Hermeneutics--Religious aspects--Comparative studies.
I. Fox, Leonard. II. Corbin, Henry. Herméneutique spirituelle comparée. English.
III. Title. IV. Series
BP189.7.174C6713 1995
289.4'092–dc20 94-30687 CIP

Edited by Barbara Phillips
Designed by Joanna V. Hill
Printed in the United States of America.

SWEDENBORG FOUNDATION
320 North Church Street • West Chester, PA 19380
www.swedenborg.com

Contents

Translator's Preface

Among the many scholars in diverse disciplines who have studied the Writings of Swedenborg over the past two centuries, Henry Corbin occupies a unique place. Universally considered to be one of the greatest Islamicists of this century, Corbin held the chair in Islam at the Sorbonne from 1954 to 1974. During this time he also organized and served as the director of the department of Iranic studies at the Institut franco-iranien in Teheran. At the time of his death, in 1978, Corbin's legacy included a large number of original books and articles, as well as numerous editions in Persian of important Sufi and Isma'ili authors. Several of his major works have been translated into English: *Creative Imagination in the Sufism of Ibn 'Arabi*; *Avicenna and the Visionary Recital*; *Spiritual Body and Celestial Earth: From Mazdean Iran to Shi'ite Iran*; *The Man of Light in Iranian Sufism*; *Temple and Contemplation*; *History of Islamic Philosophy*; and *Cyclical Time and Ismaili Gnosis.*

Although Corbin's primary interest was the esoteric tradition in Islam, he also studied the Writings of Swedenborg for many years, and he frequently mentions aspects of Swedenborg's theological system in his books on Sufi and Isma'ili subjects. Corbin once wrote that he had "plunged into the reading of Swedenborg, whose enormous work has been my companion throughout my entire life." In a personal letter to Dr. Friedemann Horn, director of the Swedenborg Verlag in Zurich, who very kindly provided me with a copy, Corbin states that he often had occasion to speak with his Shi'ite friends in Iran about Swedenborg.

The significance of Swedenborg to Corbin—and to the great Zen master Daisetz Teitaro Suzuki—is well illustrated by the fact that the following footnote appears in *Creative Imagination in the Sufism of Ibn 'Arabi* (Princeton: Princeton University Press, 1969, pp. 354–355):

> Here I should like to mention a conversation, which strikes me as memorable, with D.T. Suzuki, the master of Zen Buddhism (Casa Gabriella, Ascona, August 18, 1954, in the presence of Mrs. Fröbe-Kapteyn and Mircea Eliade). We asked him what his first encounter with Occidental spirituality had been and learned that some fifty years before Suzuki had translated four of Swedenborg's works into Japanese; this had been his first contact with the West. Later on in the conversation we asked him what homologies in structure he found between Mahayana Buddhism and the cosmology of Swedenborg in respect of the symbolism and correspondences of the worlds (cf. his *Essays in Zen Buddhism*, First Series, p. 54, n.). Of course we expected not a theoretical answer, but a sign attesting the encounter in a concrete person of an experience common to Buddhism and to Swedenborgian spirituality. And I can still see Suzuki suddenly brandishing a spoon and saying with a smile: "This spoon *now* exists in Paradise . . . ." "We are *now* in Heaven," he explained. This was an authentically Zen way of answering the question; Ibn 'Arabi would have relished it. In reference to the establishment of the transfigured world to which we have alluded above, it may not be irrelevant to mention the importance which, in the ensuing conversation, Suzuki attached to the Spirituality of Swedenborg, "your Buddha of the North."

Corbin's quite evident respect for the Writings of Swedenborg as constituting one of the highest points in religious history found greatest expression in his lengthy article

"Herméneutique spirituelle comparée (I. Swedenborg — II. Gnose ismaélienne)," originally published in 1964 in *Eranos* and reprinted in a posthumous collection of Corbin's essays entitled *Face de Dieu, face de l'homme* (Paris: Flammarion, 1984, pp. 41–162). It is interesting that in this essay Corbin again mentions the conversation with Suzuki quoted above: "And he [Suzuki] added: 'It is he [Swedenborg] who is your Buddha, for you Westerners, it is he who should be read and followed!'" (p. 45, n. 4).

In his article Corbin attempts a comparison between two esoteric hermeneutic traditions, that is, the revelation of the internal sense of the sacred books of two distinct religions, Christianity and Islam. Swedenborg, he says, "was truly, in his immense work, the prophet of the internal sense of the Bible," while "the entire Shi'ite religious phenomenon . . . rests essentially on the spiritual hermeneutics of the Qur'ān, on the esoteric sense of the prophetic Revelations."

As an introduction to this comparative study, I felt it useful to translate another of Corbin's articles (also published in *Face de Dieu, face de l'homme*), in which he discusses his use of the term that he himself invented, *mundus imaginalis*, "the *imaginal* world," which has now been adopted by many writers on Sufism and Shi'ite esoterism. This article not only clarifies an extremely important concept in both Swedenborgian and esoteric Islamic spirituality, it also vividly illustrates Corbin's own relationship to the spiritual truths that he devoted his life to elucidating.

Finally, a word on the nature of this translation. Because Corbin—a superb translator himself—chooses his words with great care and precision, I have endeavored to remain as faithful as possible to his original texts, even where this has involved producing lengthy sentences of considerable complexity. Corbin's style is undeniably complex, as is his subject matter; his work requires attentive, thoughtful reading. As far as individual words are concerned, I have chosen to translate *sensible* as "sensory" rather than "sensible," since the latter word in English has far too many meanings that are irrelevant to the context of these studies; and I have used the word "theosopher" rather than "theosophist" to translate *théosophe*, in order to avoid any possible misconstruction or association with the ideas of the Theosophical Society. I have also retained several of Corbin's innovative expressions, such as "symbolize with," instead of using the lengthier phrase "in symbolic relationship with."

Quotations from the theological writings of Emanuel Swedenborg are drawn from the standard edition published by the Swedenborg Foundation, West Chester, Pennsylvania.

LEONARD FOX
Bryn Athyn, Pennsylvania

Swedenborg
and Esoteric Islam

Mundus Imaginalis, or the Imaginary and the Imaginal

In offering the two Latin words ***mundus imaginalis*** as the title of this discussion, I intend to treat a precise order of reality corresponding to a precise mode of perception, because Latin terminology gives the advantage of providing us with a technical and fixed point of reference, to which we can compare the various more-or-less irresolute equivalents that our modern Western languages suggest to us.

I will make an immediate admission. The choice of these two words was imposed upon me some time ago, because it was impossible for me, in what I had to translate or say, to be satisfied with the word ***imaginary***. This is by no means a criticism addressed to those of us for whom the use of the language constrains recourse to this word, since we are trying together to reevaluate it in a positive sense. Regardless of our efforts, though, we cannot prevent the term ***imaginary***, in current usage that is not deliberate, from being equivalent to signifying ***unreal***, something that is and remains outside of being and existence—in brief, something ***utopian***. I was absolutely obliged to find another term because, for many years, I have been by vocation and profession an interpreter of Arabic and Persian texts, the purposes of which I would certainly have betrayed if I had been entirely and simply content—even with every possible precaution—with the term *imaginary*. I was absolutely obliged to find another term if I did not want to mislead the Western reader that it is a matter of uprooting long-established habits of thought, in order to awaken him to an order of things, the sense of which it is the mission of our colloquia at the "Society of Symbolism" to rouse.

In other words, if we usually speak of the *imaginary* as the unreal, the utopian, this must contain the symptom of something. In contrast to this something, we may examine briefly together the order of reality that I designate as *mundus imaginalis*, and what our theosophers in Islam designate as the "eighth climate"; we will then examine the organ that perceives this reality, namely, the imaginative consciousness, the *cognitive* Imagination; and finally, we will present several examples, among many others, of course, that suggest to us the topography of these interworlds, as they have been seen by those who *actually* have been there.

I. "Nā-kojā-Ābād" or the "Eighth Climate"

I have just mentioned the word *utopian*. It is a strange thing, or a decisive example, that our authors use a term in Persian that seems to be its linguistic calque: *Nā-kojā-Ābād*, the "land of No-where." This, however, is something entirely different from a *utopia*.

Let us take the very beautiful tales—simultaneously visionary tales and tales of spiritual initiation—composed in Persian by Sohravardī, the young shaykh who, in the twelfth century, was the "reviver of the theosophy of ancient Persia" in Islamic Iran. Each time, the visionary finds himself, at the beginning of the tale, in the presence of a supernatural figure of great beauty, whom the visionary asks *who* he is and from *where* he comes. These tales essentially illustrate the experience of the gnostic, lived as the personal history of the Stranger, the captive who aspires to return home.

At the beginning of the tale that Sohravardī entitles "The Crimson Archangel,"[1] the captive, who has just escaped the surveillance of his jailers, that is, has temporarily left the world of sensory experience, finds himself in the desert in the presence of a being whom he asks, since he sees in him all the charms of adolescence, "O Youth! where do you come from?" He receives this reply: "What? I am the first-born of the children of the Creator [in gnostic terms, the *Protoktistos*, the First-Created] and you call me a youth?" There, in this origin, is the mystery of the crimson color that clothes his appearance: that of a being of pure Light whose splendor the sensory world reduces to the crimson of twilight. "I come from beyond the mountain of Qāf. . . . It is there that you were yourself at the beginning, and it is there that you will return when you are finally rid of your bonds."

The mountain of Qāf is the cosmic mountain constituted from summit to summit, valley to valley, by the celestial Spheres that are enclosed one inside the other. What, then, is the road that leads out of it? How long is it? "No matter how long you walk," he is told, "it is at the point of departure that you arrive there again," like the point of the compass returning to the same place. Does this involve simply leaving oneself in order to attain oneself? Not exactly. Between the two, a great event will have changed everything; the *self* that is found there is the one that is beyond the mountain of Qāf, a superior self, a *self* "in the second person." It will have been necessary, like Khezr (or Khaḍir, the mysterious prophet, the eternal wanderer, Elijah or one like him) to bathe in the Spring of Life. "He who has found the meaning of True Reality has arrived at that Spring. When he emerges from the Spring, he has achieved the Aptitude that makes him like a balm, a drop of which you distill in the hollow of your hand by holding it facing the sun, and which then passes through to the back of your hand. If you are Khezr, you also may pass without difficulty through the mountain of Qāf."

Two other mystical tales give a name to that "beyond the mountain of Qāf," and it is this name itself that marks the transformation from cosmic mountain to *psychocosmic* mountain, that is, the transition of the physical cosmos to what constitutes the first level of the spiritual universe. In the tale entitled "The Rustling of Gabriel's Wings," the figure again appears who, in the works of Avicenna, is named *Hayy ibn Yaqzān* ("the Living, son of the Watchman") and who, just now, was designated as the Crimson Archangel. The question that must be asked is asked, and the reply is this: "I come from *Nā-kojā-Ābād*."[2] Finally, in the tale entitled "Vade Mecum of the Faithful in Love" (*Mu'nis al-'oshshāq*), which places on stage a cosmogonic triad whose dramatis personae are, respectively, Beauty, Love, and Sadness, Sadness appears to Ya'qūb weeping for Joseph in the land of Canaan. To the question, "What horizon did you penetrate to come here?," the same reply is given: "I come from *Nā-kojā-Ābād*."

Nā-kojā-Ābād is a strange term. It does not occur in any Persian dictionary, and it was coined, as far as I know, by Sohravardī himself, from the resources of the purest Persian language. Literally, as I mentioned a moment ago, it signifies the city, the country or land (*ābād*) of No-where (*Nā-kojā*). That is why we are here in the presence of a term that, at first sight, may appear to us as the exact equivalent of the term *ou-topia*, which, for its part, does not occur in the classical Greek dictionaries, and was coined by Thomas More as an abstract noun to designate the absence of any localization, of any given *situs* in a space that is discoverable and verifiable by the experience of our senses. Etymologically and literally, it would perhaps be exact to translate *Nā-kojā-Ābād* by *outopia*, utopia, and yet with regard to the concept, the intention, and the true meaning, I believe that we would be guilty of mistranslation. It seems to me, therefore, that it is of fundamental importance to try, at least, to determine why this would be a mistranslation.

It is even a matter of indispensable precision, if we want to understand the meaning and the real implication of manifold information concerning the topographies explored in the visionary state, the state intermediate between waking and sleep—information that, for example, among the spiritual individuals of Shi'ite Islam, concerns the "land of the hidden Imām." A matter of precision that, in making us attentive to a differential affecting an entire region of the soul, and thus an entire spiritual culture, would lead us to ask: what conditions make possible that which *we* ordinarily call a utopia, and consequently the type of utopian man? How and why does it make its appearance? I wonder, in fact, whether the equivalent would be found anywhere in Islamic thought in its *traditional* form. I do not believe, for example, that when Fārābī, in the tenth century, describes the "Perfect City," or when the Andalusian philosopher Ibn Bājja (Avempace), in the twelfth century, takes up the same theme in his "Regime of the Solitary"[3] —I do not believe that either one of them contemplated what we call today a social or political utopia. To understand them in this way would be, I am afraid, to withdraw them from their own presuppositions and perspectives, in order to impose our own, our own dimensions; above all, I am afraid that it would be certain to entail resigning ourselves to confusing the Spiritual City with an imaginary City.

The word *Nā-kojā-Ābād* does not designate something like unextended being, in the dimensionless state. The Persian word *ābād* certainly signifies a *city*, a cultivated and peopled land, thus something extended. What Sohravardī means by being "beyond the mountain of Qāf" is that he himself, and with him the entire theosophical tradition of Iran, represents the composite of the mystical cities of Jābalqā, Jābarsā, and Hūrqalyā. Topographically, he states precisely that this region begins "on the convex surface" of the Ninth Sphere, the Sphere of Spheres, or the Sphere that includes the whole of the cosmos. This means that it begins at the exact moment when one leaves the supreme

Sphere, which defines all possible orientation in our world (or on this side of the world), the "Sphere" to which the celestial cardinal points refer. It is evident that once this boundary is crossed, the question "*where?*" (*ubi, kojā*) loses its meaning, at least the meaning in which it is asked in the space of our sensory experience. Thus the name *Nā-kojā-Ābād*: a place outside of place, a "place" that is not contained in a place, in a *topos*, that permits a response, with a gesture of the hand, to the question "*where?*" But when we say, "To depart from the *where*," what does this mean?

It surely cannot relate to a change of local position,[4] a physical transfer from one place to another place, as though it involved places contained in a single homogeneous space. As is suggested, at the end of Sohravardī's tale, by the symbol of the drop of balm exposed in the hollow of the hand to the sun, it is a matter of entering, passing into the interior and, in passing *into the interior*, of finding oneself, paradoxically, *outside*, or, in the language of our authors, "on the convex surface" of the Ninth Sphere—in other words, "beyond the mountain of Qāf." The relationship involved is essentially that of the external, the visible, the exoteric (in Greek, τὰ ἔξω; Arabic, *ẓāhir*), and the internal, the invisible, the esoteric (in Greek τὰ ἔσω; Arabic *bāṭin*), or the natural world and the spiritual world. To depart from the *where*, the category of *ubi*, is to leave the external or natural appearances that enclose the hidden internal realities, as the almond is hidden beneath the shell. This step is made in order for the Stranger, the gnostic, to return *home*—or at least to lead to that return.

But an odd thing happens: once this transition is accomplished, it turns out that henceforth this reality, previously internal and hidden, is revealed to be enveloping, surrounding, containing what was first of all external and visible, since by means of *interiorization*, one has *departed* from that *external* reality. Henceforth, it is spiritual reality that envelops, surrounds, contains the reality called material. That is why spiritual reality is not "in the *where*." It is the "*where*" that is in it. Or, rather, it is itself the "*where*" of all things; it is, therefore, not itself in a place, it does not fall under the question "*where?*"—the category *ubi* referring to a place *in* sensory space. Its place (its *ābād*) in relation to this is *Nā-kojā* (No-where), because its *ubi* in relation to what is *in* sensory space is an *ubique* (everywhere). When we have understood this, we have perhaps understood what is essential to follow the topography of visionary experiences, to distinguish their meaning (that is, the signification and the direction simultaneously) and also to distinguish something fundamental, namely, what differentiates the visionary perceptions of our spiritual individuals (Sohravardī and many others) with regard to everything that our modern vocabulary subsumes under the pejorative sense of creations, imaginings, even *utopian* madness.

But what we must begin to destroy, to the extent that we are able to do so, even at the cost of a struggle resumed every day, is what may be called the "agnostic reflex" in Western man, because he has consented to the divorce between *thought* and *being*. How many recent theories tacitly originate in this reflex, thanks to which we hope to escape the *other* reality before which certain experiences and certain evidence place us—and to escape it, in the case where we secretly submit to its attraction, by giving it all sorts of ingenious explanations, except one: the one that would permit it truly to mean for us, by its existence, what it *is*! For it to mean that to us, we must, at all events, have available a cosmology of such a kind that the most astounding information of modern science regarding the physical universe remains inferior to it. For, insofar as it is a matter of that sort of information, we remain bound to what is "on this side of the mountain of Qāf." What distinguishes the traditional cosmology of the theosophers in Islam, for example, is that its structure—where the worlds and interworlds "beyond the mountain of Qāf," that is, beyond the physical universes, are arranged in levels—is intelligible only for an existence in which the *act of being* is in accordance with its *presence* in those worlds, for reciprocally, it is in accordance with this act of being that these worlds are present to it.[5] What dimension, then, must this *act of being* have in order to be, or to become in the course of its future rebirths, the *place* of those worlds that are *outside the place* of our natural space? And, first of all, what are those worlds?

I can only refer here to a few texts. A larger number will be found translated and grouped in the book that I have entitled *Spiritual Body and Celestial Earth*.[6] In his "Book of Conversations," Sohravardī writes: "When you learn in the treatises of the ancient Sages that there exists a world provided with dimensions and extension, other than the pleroma of Intelligences [that is, a world below that of the pure archangelic Intelligences], and other than the world governed by the Souls of the Spheres [that is, a world which, while having dimension and extension, is other than the world of sensory phenomena, and superior to it, including the sidereal universe, the planets and the "fixed stars"], a world where there are cities whose number it is impossible to count, cities among which our Prophet himself named Jābalqā and Jābarsā, do not hasten to call it a lie, for pilgrims of the spirit may contemplate that world, and they find there everything that is the object of their desire."[7]

These few lines refer us to a schema on which all of our mystical theosophers agree, a schema that articulates three universes or, rather, three categories of universe. There is our physical sensory world, which includes both our earthly world (governed by human souls) and the sidereal universe (governed by the Souls of the Spheres); this is the sensory world, the world of phenomena (*molk*). There is the suprasensory world of the Soul or Angel-Souls, the *Malakūt*, in which there are the mystical cities that we have just named, and which begins "on the convex surface of the Ninth Sphere." There is the universe of pure archangelic Intelligences. To these three universes correspond three organs of knowledge: the senses, the imagination, and the intellect, a triad to which corresponds the triad of anthropology: body, soul, spirit—a triad that regulates the triple growth of man, extending from this world to the resurrections in the other worlds.

We observe immediately that we are no longer reduced to the dilemma of thought and extension, to the schema of a cosmology and a gnoseology limited to the empirical world and the world of abstract understanding. Between the two is placed an intermediate world, which our authors designate as *'ālam al-mithāl*, the world of the Image, *mundus imaginalis*: a world as ontologically real as the world of the senses and the world of the intellect, a world that requires a faculty of perception belonging to it, a faculty that is a cognitive function, a *noetic* value, as fully real as the faculties of sensory perception or intellectual intuition. This faculty is the imaginative power, the one we must avoid confusing with the imagination that modern man identifies with "fantasy" and that, according to him, produces only the "imaginary." Here we are, then, simultaneously at the heart of our research and of our problem of terminology.

What is that intermediate universe? It is the one we mentioned a little while ago as being called the "eighth climate."[8] For all of our thinkers, in fact, the world of extension perceptible to the senses includes the *seven climates* of their traditional geography. But there is still another climate, represented by that world which, however, possesses extension and dimensions, forms and colors, without their being perceptible to the senses, as they are when they are properties of physical bodies. No, these dimensions, shapes, and colors are the proper object of imaginative perception or the "psycho-spiritual senses"; and that world, fully objective and real, where everything existing in the sensory world has its analogue, but not perceptible by the senses, is the world that is designated as the *eighth climate*. The term is sufficiently eloquent by itself, since it signifies a climate *outside* of climates, a place *outside* of place, outside of *where* (*Nā-kojā-Ābād*!).

The technical term that designates it in Arabic, *'ālam al-mithāl*, can perhaps also be translated by *mundus archetypus*, if ambiguity is avoided. For it is the same word that serves in Arabic to designate the Platonic Ideas (interpreted by Sohravardī in terms of Zoroastrian angelology). However, when the term refers to Platonic Ideas, it is almost always accompanied by this precise qualification: *mothol* (plural of *mithāl*) *aflātūnīya nūrānīya*, the "Platonic archetypes of light." When the term refers to the world of the eighth climate, it designates technically, on one hand, the *Archetype-Images* of individual and singular things; in this case, it relates to the *eastern* region of the eighth climate, the city of Jābalqā, where these images subsist, preexistent to and ordered before the sensory world. But on the other hand, the term also relates to the *western* region, the city of Jābarsā, as being the world or interworld in which are found the Spirits after their presence in the natural terrestrial world, and as a world in which subsist the forms of all works accomplished, the forms of our thoughts and our desires, of our presentiments and our behavior.[9] It is this composition that constitutes *'ālam al-mithāl*, the *mundus imaginalis*.

Technically, again, our thinkers designate it as the world of "Images in suspense" (*mothol mo'allaqa*). Sohravardī and his school mean by this a mode of being proper to the realities of that intermediate world, which we designate as *Imaginalia*.[10] The precise nature of this ontological status results from visionary spiritual experiences, on which Sohravardī asks that we rely fully, exactly as we rely in astronomy on the observations of Hipparchus or Ptolemy. It should be acknowledged that forms and shapes in the *mundus imaginalis* do not subsist in the same manner as empirical realities in the physical world; otherwise, anyone could perceive them. It should also be noted that they cannot subsist in the pure intelligible world, since they have extension and dimension, an "immaterial" materiality, certainly, in relation to that of the sensory world, but, in fact, their own "corporeality" and spatiality (one might think here of the expression used by Henry More, a Cambridge Platonist, *spissitudo spiritualis*, an expression that has its exact equivalent in the work of Sadrā Shīrāzī, a Persian Platonist). For the same reason, that they could have only our thought as a substratum would be excluded, as it would, at the same time, that they might be unreal, nothing; otherwise, we could not discern them, classify them into hierarchies, or make judgments about them. The existence of this intermediate world, *mundus imaginalis*, thus appears metaphysically necessary; the cognitive function of the Imagination is ordered to it; it is a world whose ontological level is above the world of the senses and below the pure intelligible world; it is more immaterial than the former and less immaterial than the latter.[11] There has always been something of major importance in this for all our mystical theosophers. Upon it depends, for them, both the validity of visionary accounts that perceive and relate "events in Heaven" and the validity of dreams, symbolic rituals, the reality of places formed by intense meditation, the reality of inspired imaginative visions, cosmogonies and theogonies, and thus, in the first place, the truth of the *spiritual sense* perceived in the imaginative data of prophetic revelations.[12]

In short, that world is the world of "subtle bodies," the idea of which proves indispensable if one wishes to describe a link between the pure spirit and the material body. It is this which relates to the designation of their mode of being as "in suspense," that is, a mode of being such that the Image or Form, since it is itself its own "matter," is independent of any substratum in which it would be immanent in the manner of an accident.[13] This means that it would not subsist as the color black, for example, subsists by means of the black object in which it is immanent. The comparison to which our authors regularly have recourse is the mode of appearance and subsistence of Images "in suspense" in a mirror. The material substance of the mirror, metal or mineral, is not the substance of the image, a substance whose image would be an accident. It is simply the "place of its appearance." This led to a general theory of epiphanic places and forms (*maẓhar*, plural *maẓāhir*) so characteristic of Sohravardī's *Eastern Theosophy*.

The active Imagination is the preeminent *mirror*, the epiphanic place of the Images of the archetypal world; that is why the theory of the *mundus imaginalis* is bound up with a theory of imaginative knowledge and imaginative function—a function truly central and mediatory, because of the median and mediatory position of the *mundus imaginalis*. It is a function that permits all the universes to *symbolize with one another* (or exist in symbolic relationship with one another) and that leads us to represent to ourselves, experimentally, that the same substantial realities assume forms corresponding respectively to each universe (for example, Jābalqā and Jābarsā correspond in the subtle world to the Elements of the physical world, while Hūrqalyā corresponds there to the Sky). It is the cognitive function of the Imagination that permits the establishment of a rigorous *analogical knowledge*, escaping the dilemma of current rationalism, which leaves only a choice between the two terms of banal dualism: either "matter" or "spirit," a dilemma that the "socialization" of consciousness resolves by substituting a choice that is no less fatal: either "history" or "myth."

This is the sort of dilemma that has never defeated those familiar with the "eighth climate," the realm of "subtle bodies," of "spiritual bodies," threshold of the *Malakūt* or world of the Soul. We understand that when they say that the world of Hūrqalyā begins "on the convex surface of the supreme Sphere," they wish to signify symbolically that this world is at the boundary where there is an inversion of the relation of interiority expressed by the preposition *in* or *within*, "in the interior of." Spiritual bodies or spiritual entities are no longer *in* a world, not even *in* their world, in the way that a material body is in its place, or is contained in another body. It is their world that is *in* them. That is why the *Theology* attributed to Aristotle, the Arabic version of the last three *Enneads* of Plotinus, which Avicenna annotated and which all of our thinkers read and meditated upon, explains that each spiritual entity is "in the totality of the sphere of its Heaven"; each subsists, certainly, independently of the other, but all are simultaneous and each is within every other one. It would be completely false to picture that other world as an undifferentiated, informal heaven. There is multiplicity, of course, but the relations of spiritual space differ from the relations of space understood ***under*** the starry Heaven, as much as the fact of being ***in*** a body differs from the fact of being "in the totality of its Heaven." That is why it can be said that "behind this world there is a Sky, an Earth, an ocean, animals, plants, and celestial men; but every being there is celestial; the spiritual entities there correspond to the human beings there, but no earthly thing is there."

The most exact formulation of all this, in the theosophical tradition of the West, is found perhaps in Swedenborg. One cannot but be struck by the concordance or convergence of the statements by the great Swedish visionary with those of Sohravardī, Ibn 'Arabi, or Ṣadrā Shīrāzī. Swedenborg explains that "all things in heaven appear, just as in the world, to be in place and in space, and yet the angels have no notion or idea of place or space." This is because "all changes of place in the spiritual world are effected by changes of state in the interiors, which means that change of place is nothing else than change of state. . . . Those are near each other who are in like states, and those are at a distance who are in unlike states; and spaces in heaven are simply the external conditions corresponding to the internal states. For the same reason the heavens are distinct from each other. . . . When anyone goes from one place to another . . . he arrives more quickly when he eagerly desires it, and less quickly when he does not, the way itself being lengthened and shortened in accordance with the desire. . . . This I have often seen to my surprise. All this again makes clear how distances, and consequently spaces, are wholly in accord with states of the interiors of angels; and this being so, no notion or idea of space can enter their thought, although there are spaces with them equally as in the world."[14]

Such a description is eminently appropriate to ***Nā-kojā-Ābād*** and its mysterious Cities. In short, it follows that there is a spiritual place and a corporeal place. The transfer of one to the other is absolutely not effected according to the laws of our homogeneous physical space. In relation to the corporeal place, the spiritual place is a *No-where*, and for the one who reaches ***Nā-kojā-Ābād*** everything occurs inversely to the evident facts of ordinary consciousness, which remains orientated to the interior of our space. For henceforth it is the ***where***, the place, that resides in the soul; it is the corporeal substance that resides in the spiritual substance; it is the soul that encloses and bears the body. This is why it is not possible to say ***where*** the spiritual place is situated; it is not situated, it is, rather, that which situates, it is ***situative***. Its ***ubi*** is an ***ubique***. Certainly, there may be topographical correspondences between the sensory world and the ***mundus imaginalis***, one symbolizing with the other. However, there is no passage from one to the other without a breach. Many accounts show us this. One sets out; at a given moment, there is a break with the geographical coordinates that can be located on our maps. But the "traveler" is not conscious of the precise moment; he does not realize it, with disquiet or wonder, until later. If he were aware of it, he could change his path at will, or he could indicate it to others. But he can only describe where he was; he cannot show the way to anyone.

II. The Spiritual Imagination

We will touch here on the decisive point for which all that precedes has prepared us, namely, the organ that permits penetration into the ***mundus imaginalis***, the migration to the "eighth climate." What is the organ by means of which that migration occurs—the migration that is the return ***ab extra ad intra*** (from the exterior to the interior), the topographical inversion (the ***intussusception***)? It is neither the senses nor the faculties of the physical organism, nor is it the pure intellect, but it is that intermediate power whose function appears as the preeminent mediator: the active Imagination. Let us be very clear when we speak of this. It is the organ that permits the transmutation of internal spiritual states into external states, into vision-events symbolizing with those internal states. It is by means of this transmutation that all progression in spiritual space is accomplished, or, rather, this transmutation is itself what spatializes that space, what causes space, proximity, distance, and remoteness to be there.

A *first postulate* is that this Imagination is a pure spiritual faculty, independent of the physical organism, and consequently is able to subsist after the disappearance of the latter. Ṣadrā Shīrāzī, among others, has expressed himself repeatedly on this point with particular forcefulness.[15] He says that just as the soul is independent of the physical material body in receiving intelligible things in act, according to its intellective power, the soul is equally independent with regard to its *imaginative power* and its *imaginative operations*. In addition, when it is separated from this world, since it continues to have its active Imagination at its service, it can perceive by itself, by its own essence and by that faculty, concrete things whose existence, as it is actualized in its knowledge and in its imagination, constitutes *eo ipso* the very form of concrete existence of those things (in other words: consciousness and its object are here ontologically inseparable). All these powers are gathered and concentrated in a single faculty, which is the active Imagination. Because it has stopped dispersing itself at the various thresholds that are the five senses of the physical body, and has stopped being solicited by the concerns of the physical body, which is prey to the vicissitudes of the external world, the imaginative perception can finally show its essential superiority over sensory perception.

"All the faculties of the soul," writes Ṣadrā Shīrāzī, "have become as though a single faculty, which is the power to configure and typify (*taswīr* and *tamthīl*); its imagination has itself become like a sensory perception of the suprasensory: its *imaginative sight* is itself like its sensory sight. Similarly, its senses of hearing, smell, taste, and touch—all these *imaginative senses*—are themselves like sensory faculties, but regulated to the suprasensory. For although *externally* the sensory faculties are five in number, each having its organ localized in the body, *internally*, in fact, all of them constitute a single *synaisthēsis* (*ḥiss moshtarik*)." The Imagination being therefore like the *currus subtilis* (in Greek *okhēma*, vehicle, or [in Proclus, Iamblichus, etc.] spiritual body) of the soul, there is an entire physiology of the "subtle body" and thus of the "resurrection body," which Ṣadrā Shīrāzī discusses in these contexts. That is why he reproaches even Avicenna for having identified these acts of posthumous imaginative perception with what happens in this life during sleep, for here, and during sleep, the imaginative power is disturbed by the organic operations that occur in the physical body. Much is required for it to enjoy its maximum of perfection and activity, freedom and purity. Otherwise, sleep would be simply an awakening in the other world. This is not the case, as is alluded to in this remark attributed sometimes to the Prophet and sometimes to the First Imām of the Shi'ites: "Humans sleep. It is when they die that they awake."

A *second postulate*, evidence for which compels recognition, is that the spiritual Imagination is a cognitive power, an organ of true knowledge. Imaginative perception and imaginative consciousness have their own *noetic* (cognitive) function and value, in relation to the world that is theirs—the world, we have said, which is the *'ālam al-mithāl*, *mundus imaginalis*, the world of the mystical cities such as Hūrqalyā, where time becomes reversible and where space is a function of desire, because it is only the external aspect of an internal state.

The Imagination is thus firmly *balanced* between two other cognitive functions: its own world *symbolizes with* the world to which the two other functions (sensory knowledge and intellective knowledge) respectively correspond. There is accordingly something like a control that keeps the Imagination from wanderings and profligacy, and that permits it to assume its full function: to cause the occurrence, for example, of the events that are related by the visionary tales of Sohravardī and all those of the same kind, because every approach to the eighth climate is made by the imaginative path. It may be said that this is the reason for the extraordinary gravity of mystical epic poems written in Persian (from 'Attār to Jāmī and to Nūr 'Alī-Shāh), which constantly amplify the same archetypes in new symbols. In order for the Imagination to wander and become profligate, for it to cease fulfilling its function, which is to perceive or generate symbols leading to the internal sense, it is necessary for the *mundus imaginalis*—the proper domain of the *Malakūt*, the world of the Soul—to disappear. Perhaps it is necessary, in the West, to date the beginning of this decadence at the time when Averroism rejected Avicennian cosmology, with its intermediate angelic hierarchy of the *Animae* or *Angeli caelestes.* These *Angeli caelestes* (a hierarchy below that of the *Angeli intellectuales*) had the privilege of imaginative power in its pure state. Once the universe of these Souls disappeared, it was the imaginative function as such that was *unbalanced* and devalued. It is easy to understand, then, the advice given later by Paracelsus, warning against any confusion of the *Imaginatio vera*, as the alchemists said, with fantasy, "that cornerstone of the mad."[16]

This is the reason that we can no longer avoid the problem of terminology. How is it that we do not have in French [or in English] a common and perfectly satisfying term to express the idea of the *'ālam al-mithāl*? I have proposed the Latin *mundus imaginalis* for it, because we are obliged to avoid any confusion between what is here the *object* of imaginative or imaginant perception and what we ordinarily call the *imaginary.* This is so, because the current attitude is to oppose the real to the imaginary as though to the unreal, the utopian, as it is to confuse symbol with allegory, to confuse the exegesis of the *spiritual sense* with an allegorical interpretation. Now, every allegorical interpretation is harmless; the allegory is a sheathing, or, rather, a disguising, of something that is already known or knowable otherwise, while the appearance of an Image having the quality of a symbol is a primary phenomenon (*Urphänomen*), unconditional and irreducible, the appearance of something that cannot manifest itself otherwise to the world where we are.

Neither the tales of Sohravardī, nor the tales which in the Shi'ite tradition tell us of reaching the "land of the Hidden Imām," are imaginary, unreal, or allegorical, precisely because the eighth climate or the "land of No-where" is not what we commonly call a *utopia*. It is certainly a world that remains beyond the empirical verification of our sciences. Otherwise, anyone could find access to it and evidence for it. It is a suprasensory world, insofar as it is not perceptible except by the imaginative perception, and insofar as the events that occur in it cannot be experienced except by the imaginative or imaginant consciousness. Let us be certain that we understand, here again, that this is not a matter simply of what the language of our time calls an imagination, but of a *vision* that is *Imaginatio vera*. And it is to this *Imaginatio vera* that we must attribute a *noetic* or plenary cognitive value. If we are no longer capable of speaking about the imagination except as "fantasy," if we cannot utilize it or tolerate it except as such, it is perhaps because we have forgotten the norms and the rules and the "axial ordination" that are responsible for the *cognitive* function of the imaginative power (the function that I have sometimes designated as *imaginatory*).

For the world into which our witnesses have penetrated—we will meet two or three of those witnesses in the final section of this study—is a perfectly *real* world, more evident even and more coherent, in its own reality, than the *real* empirical world perceived by the senses. Its witnesses were afterward perfectly conscious that they had been "elsewhere"; they are not schizophrenics. It is a matter of a world that is hidden in the act itself of sensory perception, and one that we must find under the apparent objective certainty of that kind of perception. That is why we positively cannot qualify it as *imaginary*, in the current sense in which the word is taken to mean unreal, nonexistent. Just as the Latin word *origo* has given us the derivative "original," I believe that the word *imago* can give us, along with *imaginary*, and by regular derivation, the term *imaginal*. We will thus have the *imaginal* world be intermediate between the *sensory* world and the *intelligible* world. When we encounter the Arabic term *jism mithālī* to designate the "subtle body" that penetrates into the "eighth climate," or the "resurrection body," we will be able to translate it literally as *imaginal body*, but certainly not as *imaginary body*. Perhaps, then, we will have less difficulty in placing the figures who belong neither to "myth" nor to "history," and perhaps we will have a sort of password to the path to the "lost continent."

In order to embolden us on this path, we have to ask ourselves what constitutes our *real*, the *real* for us, so that if we leave it, would we have more than the imaginary, utopia? And what is the *real* for our traditional Eastern thinkers, so that they may have access to the "eighth climate," to *Nā-kojā Ābād*, by leaving the sensory place without leaving the real, or, rather, by having access precisely to the real? This presupposes a scale of being with many more degrees than ours. For let us make no mistake. It is not enough to concede that our predecessors, in the West, had a conception of the Imagination that was too rationalistic and too intellectualized. If we do not have available a cosmology whose schema can include, as does the one that belongs to our traditional philosophers, the plurality of universes in ascensional order, our Imagination will remain *unbalanced*, its recurrent conjunctions with the will to power will be an endless source of horrors. We will be continually searching for a new discipline of the Imagination, and we will have great difficulty in finding it as long as we persist in seeing in it only a certain way of keeping our ***distance*** with regard to what we call the ***real***, and in order to exert an influence on that real. Now, that real appears to us as arbitrarily limited, as soon as we compare it to the real that our traditional theosophers have glimpsed, and that limitation degrades the reality itself. In addition, it is always the word ***fantasy*** that appears as an excuse: literary fantasy, for example, or preferably, in the taste and style of the day, social fantasy.

But it is impossible to avoid wondering whether the ***mundus imaginalis***, in the proper meaning of the term, would of necessity be lost and leave room only for the imaginary if something like a secularization of the ***imaginal*** into the ***imaginary*** were not required for the fantastic, the horrible, the monstrous, the macabre, the miserable, and the absurd to triumph. On the other hand, the art and imagination of Islamic culture in its traditional form are characterized by the hieratic and the serious, by gravity, stylization, and meaning. Neither our utopias, nor our science fiction, nor the sinister "***omega*** point"—nothing of that kind succeeds in leaving this world or attaining ***Nā-kojā-Ābād***. Those who have known the "eighth climate" have not invented utopias, nor is the ultimate thought of Shi'ism a social or political fantasy, but it is an eschatology, because it is an ***expectation*** which is, as such, a ***real Presence*** here and now in another world, and a testimony to that other world.

III. Topographies of the "Eighth Climate"

We ought here to examine the extensive theory of the witnesses to that other world. We ought to question all those mystics who, in Islam, repeated the visionary experience of the heavenly assumption of the Prophet Muḥammad (the ***mi'rāj***), which offers more than one feature in common with the account, preserved in an old gnostic book, of the celestial visions of the prophet Isaiah. There, the activity of imaginative perception truly assumes the aspect of a *hierognosis,* a higher sacral knowledge. But in order to complete our discussion, I will limit myself to describing several features typical of accounts taken from Shi'ite literature, because the world into which it will allow us to penetrate seems, at first sight, still to be our world, while in fact the events take place in the eighth climate—not in the imaginary, but in the imaginal world, that is, the world whose coordinates cannot be plotted on our maps, and where the Twelfth Imām, the "Hidden Imām," lives a mysterious life surrounded by his companions, who are veiled under the same incognito as the Imām. One of the most typical of these accounts is the tale of a voyage to "the Green Island situated in the White Sea."

It is impossible to describe here, even in broad terms, what constitutes the essence of Shi'ite Islam in relation to what is appropriately called Sunni orthodoxy. It is necessary, however, that we should have, at least allusively present in mind, the theme that dominates the horizon of the mystical theosophy of Shi'ism, namely, the "eternal prophetic Reality" (*Ḥaqīqat moḥammadīya*) that is designated as "Muḥammadan Logos" or "Muḥammadan Light" and is composed of fourteen entities of light: the Prophet, his daughter Fātima, and the twelve Imāms. This is the pleroma of the "Fourteen Pure Ones," by means of whose countenance the mystery of an eternal theophany is accomplished from world to world. Shi'ism has thus given Islamic prophetology its metaphysical foundation at the same time that it has given it Imāmology as the absolutely necessary complement. This means that the sense of the Divine Revelations is not limited to the letter, to the exoteric that is the cortex and containant, and that was enunciated by the Prophet; the true sense is the hidden internal, the esoteric, what is symbolized by the cortex, and which it is incumbent upon the Imāms to reveal to their followers. That is why Shi'ite theosophy eminently possesses the sense of symbols.

Moreover, the closed group or dynasty of the twelve Imāms is not a political dynasty in earthly competition with other political dynasties; it projects over them, in a way, as the dynasty of the guardians of the Grail, in our Western traditions, projects over the official hierarchy of the Church. The ephemeral earthly appearance of the twelve Imāms concluded with the twelfth, who, as a young child (in A.H. 260/A.D. 873) went into occultation from this world, but whose parousia the Prophet himself announced, the Manifestation at the end of our Aiōn, when he would reveal the hidden meaning of all Divine Revelations and fill the earth with justice and peace, as it will have been filled until then with violence and tyranny. Present simultaneously in the past and the future, the Twelfth Imām, the Hidden Imām, has been for ten centuries the *history* itself of Shi'ite consciousness, a history over which, of course, historical criticism loses its rights, for its events, although real, nevertheless do not have the reality of events in our climates, but they have the reality of those in the "eighth climate," events of the soul which are visions. His occultation occurred at two different times: the minor occultation (260/873) and the major occultation (330/942).[17] Since then, the Hidden Imām is in the position of those who were removed from the visible world without crossing the threshold of death: Enoch, Elijah, and Christ himself, according to the teaching of the Qur'ān. He is the Imām "hidden from the senses, but present in the heart of his followers," in the words of the consecrated formula, for he remains the mystical pole [*qoṭb*] of this world, the *pole of poles,* without whose existence the human world could not continue to exist. There is an entire Shi'ite literature about those to whom the Imām has manifested himself, or who have approached him but without seeing him, during the period of the Great Occultation.

Of course, an understanding of these accounts postulates certain premises that our preceding analyses permit us to accept. The first point is that the Imām lives in a mysterious place that is by no means among those that empirical geography can verify; it cannot be situated on our maps. This place "outside of place" nonetheless has its own topography. The second point is that life is not limited to the conditions of our visible material world with its biological laws that we know. There are events in the life of the Hidden Imām—even descriptions of his five sons, who are the governors of mysterious cities. The third point is that in his last letter to his last visible representative, the Imām warned against the imposture of people who would pretend to quote him, to have seen him, in order to lay claim to a public or political role in his name. But the Imām never excluded the fact that he would manifest himself to aid someone in material or moral distress—a lost traveler, for example, or a believer who is in despair

These manifestations, however, never occur except at the initiative of the Imām; and if he appears most often in the guise of a young man of supernatural beauty, almost always, subject to exception, the person granted the privilege of this vision is only conscious afterward, later, of whom he has seen. A strict incognito covers these manifestations; that is why the religious event here can never be socialized. The same incognito covers the Imām's companions, that elite of elites composed of young people in his service. They form an esoteric hierarchy of a strictly limited number, which remains permanent by means of substitution from generation to generation. This mystical order of knights, which surrounds the Hidden Imām, is subject to an incognito as strict as that of the knights of the Grail, inasmuch as they do not lead anyone to themselves. But someone who has been led there will have penetrated for a moment into the eighth climate; for a moment he will have been "in the totality of the Heaven of his soul."

That was indeed the experience of a young Iranian shaykh, 'Ali ibn Fāzel Māzandarānī, toward the end of our thirteenth century, an experience recorded in the *Account of strange and*

marvelous things that he contemplated and saw with his own eyes on the Green Island situated in the White Sea. I can only give a broad outline of this account here, without going into the details that guarantee the means and authenticity of its transmission.[18] The narrator himself gives a long recital of the years and circumstances of his life preceding the event; we are dealing with a scholarly and spiritual personality who has both feet on the ground. He tells us how he emigrated, how in Damascus he followed the teaching of an Andalusian shaykh, and how he became attached to this shaykh; and when the latter left for Egypt, he together with a few other disciples accompanied him. From Cairo he followed him to Andalusia, where the shaykh had suddenly been called by a letter from his dying father. Our narrator had scarcely arrived in Andalusia when he contracted a fever that lasted for three days. Once recovered, he went into the village and saw a strange group of men who had come from a region near the land of the Berbers, not far from the "peninsula of the Shi'ites." He is told that the journey takes twenty-five days, with a large desert to cross. He decides to join the group. Up to this point, we are still more or less on the geographical map.

But it is no longer at all certain that we are still on it when our traveler reaches the peninsula of the Shi'ites, a peninsula surrounded by four walls with high massive towers; the outside wall borders the coast of the sea. He asks to be taken to the principal mosque. There, for the first time, he hears, during the muezzin's call to prayer, resounding from the minaret of the mosque, the Shi'ite invocation asking that "Joy should hasten," that is, the joy of the future Appearance of the Imām, who is now hidden. In order to understand his emotion and his tears, it is necessary to think of the heinous persecutions, over the course of many centuries and over vast portions of the territory of Islam, that reduced the Shi'ites, the followers of the holy Imāms, to a state of secrecy. Recognition among Shi'ites is effected here again in the observation, in a typical manner, of the customs of the "discipline of the arcanum."

Our pilgrim takes up residence among his own, but he notices in the course of his walks that there is no sown field in the area. Where do the inhabitants obtain their food? He learns that food comes to them from "the Green Island situated in the White Sea," which is one of the islands belonging to the sons of the Hidden Imām. Twice a year, a flotilla of seven ships brings it to them. That year the first voyage had already taken place; it would be necessary to wait four months until the next voyage. The account describes the pilgrim passing his days, overwhelmed by the kindness of the inhabitants, but in an anguish of expectation, walking tirelessly along the beach, always watching the high sea, toward the west, for the arrival of the ships. We might be tempted to believe that we are on the African coast of the Atlantic and that the Green Island belongs, perhaps, to the Canaries or the "Fortunate Isles." The details that follow will suffice to undeceive us. Other traditions place the Green Island elsewhere—in the Caspian Sea, for example—as though to indicate to us that it has no coordinates in the geography of this world.

Finally, as if according to the law of the "eighth climate" ardent desire has shortened space, the seven ships arrive somewhat in advance and make their entry into the port. From the largest of the ships descends a shaykh of noble and commanding appearance, with a handsome face and magnificent clothes. A conversation begins, and our pilgrim realizes with astonishment that the shaykh already knows everything about him, his name and his origin. The shaykh is his Companion, and he tells him that he has come to find him: together they will leave for the Green Island. This episode bears a characteristic feature of the gnostic's feeling everywhere and always: he is an exile, separated from his own people, whom he barely remembers, and he has still less an idea of the way that will take him back to them. One day, though, a message arrives from them, as in the "Song of the Pearl" in the *Acts of Thomas,* as in the "Tale of Western Exile" by Sohravardī. Here, there is something better than a message: it is one of the companions of the Imām in person. Our narrator exclaims movingly: "Upon hearing these words, I was overwhelmed with happiness. *Someone remembered me, my name was known to them!*" Was his exile at an end? From now on, he is entirely certain that the itinerary cannot be transferred onto our maps.

The crossing lasts sixteen days, after which the ship enters an area where the waters of the sea are completely white; the Green Island is outlined on the horizon. Our pilgrim learns from his Companion that the White Sea forms an uncrossable zone of protection around the island; no ship manned by the enemies of the Imām and his people can venture there without the waves engulfing it. Our travelers land on the Green Island. There is a city at the edge of the sea; seven walls with high towers protect the precincts (this is the preeminent symbolic plan). There are luxuriant vegetation and abundant streams. The buildings are constructed from diaphanous marble. All the inhabitants have beautiful and young faces, and they wear magnificent clothes. Our Iranian shaykh feels his heart fill with joy, and from this point on, throughout the entire second part, his account will take on the rhythm and the meaning of an *initiation account,* in which we can distinguish three phases. There is an initial series of conversations with a noble personage who is none other than a grandson of the Twelfth Imām (the son of one of his five sons), and who governs the Green Island: Sayyed Shamsoddīn. These conversations compose a first initiation into the secret of the Hidden Imām; they take place sometimes in the shadow of a mosque and sometimes in the serenity of gardens filled with perfumed trees of all kinds. There follows a visit to a mysterious sanctuary in the heart of the mountain that is the highest peak on the island. Finally, there is a concluding series of conversations of decisive importance with regard to the possibility or impossibility of having a vision of the Imām.

I am giving the briefest possible summary here, and I must pass over in silence the details of scenery depiction and of an intensely animated dramaturgy, in order to note only the central episode. At the summit or at the heart of the mountain, which is in the center of the Green Island, there is a small temple, with a cupola, where one can communicate with the Imām, because it happens that he leaves a personal message there, but no one is permitted to ascend to this temple except Sayyed Shamsoddīn and those who are like him. This small temple stands in the shadow of the *Tūbā* tree; now, we know that this is the name of the tree that shades Paradise; it is the *Tree of Being*. The temple is at the edge of a spring, which, since it gushes at the base of the Tree of Paradise, can only be the *Spring of Life*. In order to confirm this for us, our pilgrim meets there the incumbent of this temple, in whom we recognize the mysterious prophet Khezr (Khaḍir). It is there, at the heart of being, in the shade of the Tree and at the edge of the Spring, that the sanctuary is found where the Hidden Imām may be most closely approached. Here we have an entire constellation of easily recognizable archetypal symbols.

We have learned, among other things, that access to the little mystical temple was only permitted to a person who, by attaining the spiritual degree at which the Imām has become his personal internal Guide, has attained a state "similar" to that of the actual descendant of the Imām. This is why the idea of internal conformation is truly at the center of the initiation account, and it is this that permits the pilgrim to learn other secrets of the Green Island: for example, the symbolism of a particularly eloquent ritual.[19] In the Shi'ite liturgical calendar, Friday is the weekday especially dedicated to the Twelfth Imām. Moreover, in the lunar calendar, the middle of the month marks the midpoint of the lunar cycle, and the middle of the month of Sha'bān is the anniversary date of the birth of the Twelfth Imām into this world. On a Friday, then, while our Iranian pilgrim is praying in the mosque, he hears a great commotion outside. His initiator, Sayyed, informs him that each time the day of the ***middle of the month*** falls on a Friday, the chiefs of the mysterious militia that surrounds the Imām assemble in "expectation of Joy," a consecrated term, as we know, which means: in the expectation of the Manifestation of the Imām in this world. Leaving the mosque, he sees a gathering of horsemen from whom a triumphal clamor rises. These are the 313 chiefs of the supernatural order of knights always present incognito in this world, in the service of the Imām. This episode leads us gradually to the final scenes that precede the farewell. Like a leitmotiv, the expression of the desire to see the Imām returns ceaselessly. Our pilgrim will learn that twice in his life he was in the Imām's presence: he was lost in the desert and the Imām came to his aid. But as is an almost constant rule, he knew nothing of it then; he learns of it now that he has come to the Green Island. Alas, he must leave this island; the order cannot be rescinded; the ships are waiting, the same one on which he arrived. But even more than for the voyage outward, it is impossible for us to mark out the itinerary that leads from the "eighth climate" to this world. Our traveler obliterates his tracks, but he will keep some material evidence of his sojourn: the pages of notes taken in the course of his conversations with the Imām's grandson, and the parting gift from the latter at the moment of farewell.

The account of the Green Island allows us an abundant harvest of symbols: (1) It is one of the islands belonging to the sons of the Twelfth Imām. (2) It is that island, where the Spring of Life gushes, in the shade of the Tree of Paradise, that ensures the sustenance of the Imām's followers who live far away, and that sustenance can only be a "suprasubstantial" food. (3) It is situated in the west, as the city of Jābarsā is situated in the west of the *mundus imaginalis,* and thus it offers a strange analogy with the paradise of the East, the paradise of Amitābha in Pure Land Buddhism; similarly, the figure of the Twelfth Imām is suggestive of comparison with Maitreya, the future Buddha; there is also an analogy with Tir-na'n-Og, one of the worlds of the Afterlife among the Celts, the land of the West and the forever young. (4) Like the domain of the Grail, it is an interworld that is self-sufficient. (5) It is protected against and immune to any attempt from outside. (6) Only one who is summoned there can find the way. (7) A mountain rises in the center; we have noted the symbols that it conceals. (8) Like Mont-Salvat, the inviolable Green Island is the place where his followers approach the mystical *pole* of the world, the Hidden Imām, reigning invisibly over this age— the jewel of the Shi'ite faith.

This tale is completed by others, for, as we have mentioned, nothing has been said until now about the islands under the reign of the truly extraordinary figures who are the five sons of the Hidden Imām (homologues of those whom Shi'ism designates as the "Five Personages of the Mantle"[20] and perhaps also of those whom Manichaeism designates as the "Five Sons of the Living Spirit"). An earlier tale[21] (it is from the middle of the twelfth century and the narrator is a Christian) provides us with complementary topographical information. Here again it involves travelers who suddenly realize that their ship has entered a completely unknown area. They land at a first island, *al-Mobāraka*, the Blessed City. Certain difficulties, brought about by the presence among them of Sunni Muslims, oblige them to travel farther. But their captain refuses; he is afraid of the unknown region. They have to hire a new crew. In succession, we learn the names of the five islands and the names of those who govern them: *al-Zāhera,* the City Blooming with Flowers; *al-Rā'yeqa,* the Limpid City; *al-Sāfiya,* the Serene City, etc. Whoever manages to gain admittance to them enters into joy forever. Five islands, five cities, five sons of the Imām, twelve months to travel through the islands (two months for each of the first four, four months for the fifth), all of these numbers having a symbolic significance. Here, too, the tale turns into an initiation account; all the travelers finally embrace the Shi'ite faith.

As there is no rule without an exception, I will conclude by citing in condensed form a tale illustrating a case of manifestation of the Imām in person.[22] The tale is from the tenth century. An Iranian from Hamadān made the pilgrimage to Mecca. On the way back, a day's journey from Mecca (more than two thousand kilometers from Hamadān), having imprudently gone astray during the night, he loses his companions. In the morning he is wandering alone in the desert and placing his trust in God. Suddenly, he sees a garden that neither he nor anyone else has ever heard of. He enters it. At the door of a pavilion, two young pages dressed in white await him and lead him to a young man of supernatural beauty. To his fearful and awestruck astonishment, he learns that he is in the presence of the Twelfth Imām. The latter speaks to him about his future Appearance and finally, addressing him by name, asks him whether he wants to return to his home and family. Certainly, he wants to do so. The Imām signals to one of his pages, who gives the traveler a purse, takes him by the hand, and guides him through the gardens. They walk together until the traveler sees a group of houses, a mosque, and shade trees that seem familiar to him. Smiling, the page asks him: "Do you know this land?" "Near where I live in Hamadān," he replies, "there is a land called Asadābād, which exactly resembles this place." The page says to him, "But *you are in Asadābād."* Amazed, the traveler realizes that he is actually near his home. He turns around; the page is no longer there, he is all alone, but he still has in his hand the viaticum that had been given to him. Did we not say a little while ago that the *where,* the *ubi,* of the "eighth climate" is an *ubique?*

I know how many commentaries can be applied to these tales, depending upon whether we are metaphysicians, traditionalist or not, or whether we are psychologists. But by way of provisional conclusion, I prefer to limit myself to asking three small questions:

1. We are no longer participants in a traditional culture; we live in a scientific civilization that is extending its control, it is said, even to images. It is commonplace today to speak of a "civilization of the image" (thinking of our magazines, cinema, and television). But one wonders whether, like all commonplaces, this does not conceal a radical misunderstanding, a complete er-

ror. For instead of the image being elevated to the level of a world that would be proper to it, instead of it appearing invested with a *symbolic function,* leading to an internal sense, there is above all a reduction of the image to the level of sensory perception pure and simple, and thus a definitive degradation of the image. Should it not be said, therefore, that the more successful this reduction is, the more the sense of the *imaginal* is lost, and the more we are condemned to producing only the *imaginary*?

2. In the second place, all imagery, the scenic perspective of a tale like the voyage to the Green Island, or the sudden encounter with the Imām in an unknown oasis—would all this be possible without the absolutely primary and irreducible, objective, initial fact (*Urphänomen*) of a world of image-archetypes or image-sources whose origin is nonrational and whose incursion into our world is unforeseeable, but whose postulate compels recognition?

3. In the third place, is it not precisely this postulate of the objectivity of the *imaginal world* that is suggested to us, or imposed on us, by certain forms or certain symbolic emblems (hermetic, kabbalistic; or *mandalas*) that have the quality of effecting a magic display of mental images, such that they assume an objective reality?

To indicate in what sense it is possible to have an idea of how to respond to the question concerning the *objective* reality of supernatural figures and encounters with them, I will simply refer to an extraordinary text, where Villiers de L'Isle-Adam speaks about the face of the inscrutable Messenger with eyes of clay; it "could not be perceived except by the spirit. Creatures experience only influences that are inherent in the archangelic entity. "Angels," he writes, "*are not,* in substance, except in the free sublimity of the absolute Heavens, where reality is unified with the ideal.... They only externalize themselves in the ecstasy they cause and which forms a part of themselves."[23]

Those last words, *an ecstasy . . . which forms part of themselves,* seem to me to possess a prophetic clarity, for they have the quality of piercing even the granite of doubt, of paralyzing the "agnostic reflex," in the sense that they break the reciprocal isolation of the consciousness and its object, of thought and being; phenomenology is now an ontology. Undoubtedly, this is the postulate implied in the teaching of our authors concerning the *imaginal.* For there is no external criterion for the manifestation of the Angel, other than the manifestation itself. The Angel is itself the *ekstasis,* the "displacement" or the departure from ourselves that is a "change of state" from our state. That is why these words also suggest to us the secret of the supernatural being of the "Hidden Imām" and of his Appearances for the Shi'ite consciousness: the Imām is the *ekstasis* itself of that consciousness. One who is not in the same spiritual state cannot see him.

This is what Sohravardī alluded to in his tale of "The Crimson Archangel" by the words that we cited at the beginning: "If you are Khezr, you also may pass without difficulty through the mountain of Qāf."

March 1964

Notes

1. *See L'Archange empourpré, quinze traités et récits mystiques,* Documents spirituels 14 (Paris: Fayard, 1976), 6: 201-213. For the entirety of the themes discussed here, see our book *En Islam iranien: Aspects spirituels et philosophiques,* new ed. (Paris: Gallimard, 1978), vol. 4, bk. 7, "Le Douzième Imām et la chevalerie spirituelle."

2. See *L'Archange empourpré,* 7: 227-239.

3. See our *Histoire de la philosophie islamique* (Paris: Gallimard, 1964), 1: 222 ff., 317 ff.

4. That is why the representation of the Sphere of Spheres in Peripatetic or Ptolemaic astronomy is only a schematic indication; it continues to be of value even after this astronomy is abandoned. This means that regardless of how "high" rockets or sputniks can reach, there will not be a single step made toward Nā-kojā-Ābād, for the "threshold" will not have been crossed.

5. Regarding this idea of presence, see particularly our introduction to Mollā Ṣadrā Shīrāzī, *Le Livre des pénétrations métaphysiques* (*Kitāb al-Mashā'ir*), edition and French translation (Bibliothèque Iranienne, vol. 10), Paris: Adrien-Maisonneuve, 1964, index under this term.

6. See our work *Spiritual Body and Celestial Earth: From Mazdean Iran to Shi'ite Iran* (Princeton: Princeton University Press, 1977), especially the texts of the eleven authors translated for the first time, in the second part of the work. The notes here refer to the second French edition, *Corps spirituel et Terre céleste: de l'Iran mazdéen à l'Iran shi'ite* (Paris: Buchet-Chastel, 1979).

7. *Corps spirituel*, p. 147.

8. For what follows, ibid., pp. 103, 106, 112 ff., 154 ff.

9. Ibid., pp. 156 ff., 190 ff.

10. Ibid., pp. 112 ff., 154 ff.

11. Ibid., p. 155

12. Ibid., p. 112.

13. Ibid., p. 113.

14. Emanuel Swedenborg, *Heaven and its Wonders and Hell*, trans. J. C. Ager (New York: Swedenborg Foundation, 1900), §§ 191 to 195. Swedenborg returns repeatedly to this doctrine of space and time—for example in the short book *Earths in the Universe*. If there is not rigorous awareness of this, his visionary experiences will be objected to by a criticism that is as simplistic as it is ineffective, because it confuses spiritual vision of the spiritual world with what relates to the fantasy of science fiction. There is an abyss between the two.

15. See our article "La place de Mollā Ṣadrā Shīrāzī (ob. 1050/1640) dans la philosophie iranienne," *Studia Islamica* (1963), as well as the work cited above, note 5.

16. See our work *L'Imagination créatrice dans le soufisme d'Ibn 'Arabī*, 2nd ed. (Paris: Flammarion, 1977), p. 139. (First edition translated as *Creative Imagination in the Sufism of Ibn 'Arabi* [Princeton: Princeton University Press, 1969].) Regarding the theory of the *Angeli caelestes*, see our book *Avicenne et le Récit visionnaire*, vol. 1, Bibliothèque Iranienne, vol. 4 (Paris: Adrien-Maisonneuve, 1954; 2nd ed., Paris: Berg international, 1982). English translation of the first edition: *Avicenna and the Visionary Recital* (Princeton: Princeton University Press, 1960).

17. For more details, see *En Islam iranien*, vol. 4, bk. 7; and our *Histoire de la philosophie islamique*, pp. 101 ff.

18. See *En Islam iranien*, vol. 4, bk. 7, pp. 346 ff.

19. Ibid., pp. 361-362.

20. Ibid., p. 373.

21. Ibid., § 3, pp. 367 ff.

22. Ibid., § 4, pp. 374 ff.

23. Villiers de L'Isle-Adam, *L'Annonciateur* (epilogue).

Comparative Spiritual Hermeneutics

Regarding the Method of Comparative Spiritual Hermeneutics

There is an Arabic term, the word *ḥikāyat*, the apparent ambiguity of which connotes simultaneously the sense of narrative, account, *history*, and that of imitation (μίμησις), as though to signify for us that the art (or the style) of the narrator, the historian, is basically that of mime. The ambiguity of the term is indicated, not without humor, when it is used to designate a grammatical point, where a word employed by an interlocutor is repeated in the reply, placing it in the same grammatical case, even if a solecism results. In order to transpose the example into a language more commonly accessible than Arabic, let us suppose that someone says to me in Latin, *"Puto eos esse Romanos,"* and, in reply, I do not say, *"Non sunt Romani,"* but *"Non sunt Romanos."* In order to "imitate" the initial form used by the interlocutor, to retain it in passing from the datum to the response, it is necessary to consent to this unusual figure that suspends grammatical law. That is a *ḥikāyat*.

It is precisely this which imbues the actual idea of *ḥikāyat* with its full significance. It is said, for example, that the procession of pilgrims around the temple of the *Ka'ba,* at Mecca, is a *ḥikāyat* of the procession of the angels "in heaven" around the celestial Temple.[1] A *ḥikāyat* is, therefore, an imitation (a *mimēsis*), a repetition, a *history* certainly, but a history that is essentially an image or symbol. It is this symbolic quality of the history that imparts, as such, an unusual form to the commonplace texture of external events; the latter are henceforth related to a higher requirement, just as, in the example given above, the *ḥikāyat* suspended the usual grammatical rule. From that point onward, it is impossible not to question the "meaning" of that history and, in general, the "meaning of all history" for a traditional culture, particularly the one that concerns us here, in the case of Islamic gnosis. This meaning cannot be anything other than the spiritual truth (the *ḥaqīqat*) of that history, and this spiritual truth cannot be glimpsed without placing oneself within a perspective altogether different from the one familiar to our modern mythology of the "meaning of history." That is why the term *ḥikāyat* seems to me to introduce best a certain way of viewing the theme that has been suggested to us this year, namely, "the human drama in the world of ideas." Because it refers all of history to another universe, this term leads us, in fact, to an immediate broadening of the suggested subject, that is, "in the Spiritual World"—the world that is at once real and invisible, not a world of abstractions and general, technocratic laws, but a concrete spiritual world, which is the place of "events in Heaven."

Since Hegel established the phenomenology of historical consciousness, we have been accustomed to placing Nature and History in contrast, with History constituting in its own right the world of man. Now, for the type of vision of the world that we will consider here, which includes everything that is closely or distantly related to Neoplatonism, the opposite of Nature is by no means History, since History, like Nature, is also part of the *physis*: it is the victim of the irreversible sequence of chronological time, of a homogeneous time that measures the revolutions of the stars; its "events" are subject to the laws of a space that disperses them far from each other, that renders them *absent* from each other. Taken as a whole, the opposite of Nature and History is to be sought in the vertical, in a world whose level dominates the level common to both Nature and History. This is the Spiritual World, which presents a highly complex structure of diversity and hierarchy.

Both the natural world and the historical world of man on earth are the *ḥikāyat*, the *mimēsis*, afflicted, alas, by an inevitable solecism, which is the *history* that is an *imitation* of the world of the Soul. Nature and History are both the visible, external, exoteric (*ẓāhir*) appearance of this spiritual world that is the hidden, the truly real (*ḥaqīqat*), the esoteric (*bāṭin*); it is in this world that true history is revealed by an approach that is called in Arabic *ta'wīl*, spiritual hermeneutics, a process that consists etymologically in "bringing back" everything, every event, to its truth, to its archetype (*aṣl*), by uncovering the hidden and concealing the appearance. It is evident that the meaning of prophethood, for example, is not in the simple material facts of the external biography of the prophets and the Imāms of Shi'ism, but it is in their spiritual meaning, that is, in the events that happen to them, invisibly, in the world of the Spirit. Externally, these events have a natural framework, human scenery. Nature, too, is a *Liber mundi*, the hidden meaning of which must be deciphered by *ta'wīl*, just as by means of *ta'wīl* the spiritual meaning of the *Liber revelatus* is unveiled, the true meaning of the Book that "decended from Heaven" and thus the secret of the prophets, that is, that of *hierohistory*.[2]

By its nature, at the heart of a prophetic religion—that is, a religion that professes the necessity of superhuman mediators between the divinity who inspires them and humanity as a whole—there is the *phenomenon of the Sacred Book* that every prophet who has the quality of a Messenger (*morsal, rasūl*) brings to man. This phenomenon preeminently creates a "hermeneutic situation," the great issue being to know and understand the *true meaning* of the Book. It is on this point that, for a number of years, my research has drawn my attention to the common factors in the manner in which spiritual individuals, mystics or mystic theosophers, have read or read the Bible in Christianity and the Qur'ān in Islam. I do not refer in any way here to the very famous medieval theory of the four meanings of the Scriptures (literal, moral, allegorical, and anagogic); this theory, in relation to our present subject, is as inoperative as it is harmless.[3] The way of reading and comprehending to which I refer presupposes, in the strict sense of the word, a *theosophia*, that is, the mental or visionary penetration of an entire hierarchy of spiritual universes that are not discovered by means of syllogisms, because they do not reveal themselves except through a certain mode of cognition, a *hierognosis* that unites the speculative knowledge of traditional information to the most personal interior experience, for, in the absence of the latter, technical models alone would be transmitted, and these would be doomed to a rapid decline. It also happens that the truth of the hidden meaning is manifested from time to time as a new revelation under the inspiration of the Spirit; the hermeneutics are renewed; they accompany the recurrence of a certain number of archetypes, which attests in a way to the objectivity of the spiritual worlds on which these hermeneutics rely.

Only two pinnacles can be considered in the course of this discussion. In the eighteenth century, in Christianity, the great Swedish visionary theosopher Emanuel Swedenborg (1688-1772) was truly, in his immense work, the prophet of the internal sense of the Bible—and this spiritual sense has nothing to do with allegory.[4] In Islam, on the other hand, there is the entire religious phenomenon of Shi'ism, which, whether in its Twelve-Imām or Seven-Imām (Isma'ili) form, is based essentially on the spiritual hermeneutics of the Qur'ān, on the esoteric sense of the prophetic Revelations.

Of course, I am the first to recognize the complexity, to say the least, of this comparative task. We should begin, no doubt, by comparing information that is common to the Bible and the

Qur'ān regarding the history of the prophets; we should also pinpoint the differences and specify their source. In addition, we must analyze how, in both cases, owing to the spiritual hermeneutics professed, there is a tendency to construct a general theology of religions. It is certain, for example, that the Swedenborgian vision of the *Nova Hierosolyma* aspires to a loftiness of level that is not the one of official dogmatics, just as the loftiness of level of the Isma'ili hermeneutics of the Qur'ān is not the same as that of Sunni Islam. Finally, in both cases, we are concerned with spiritual hermeneutics that are rigorous, systematic, and highly complex, in full possession of method, and vivified by a spirituality that cannot be ignored if there is a true desire to understand and interpret (for that is the actual meaning of the Greek word *hermēneia*, hermeneutics).

The methodological and philosophical presuppositions of this study, however, cannot be clearly stated without applying them. On one hand, symbolic hermeneutics are developed by Swedenborg with systematic precision and admirable coherence, and applied to every detail and representation, to every person, every image of verses of the Bible. On the other hand, Shi'ite hermeneutics are developed on several planes or octaves of universes. For Isma'ilism in particular, all the events of hierohistory have agents who are members (*ḥodūd*) of secret celestial and terrestrial hierarchies; the exoteric narrative of their *acts* is only the *ḥikāyat*, the *mimēsis* of events that take place in the Spiritual World; the true nature and role of the protagonists, their activity and its meaning, escape the notice of external history and the historian of external things. Despite the complexity of these matters and the incompleteness of preliminary work, perhaps an initial result may be hoped for if we limit ourselves to the meaning discerned, in both cases, in the events that *continue* to be the beginnings of the spiritual history of man. What does the role of Adam signify? What does the departure from Paradise signify? What is the significance of the drama experienced by Noah? What do the Ark and the Flood represent? It is striking that in both cases it is proclaimed that this is not the history of a past that is closed and gone, but that it has a present significance, and that the meanings which emerge in both cases are convergent.

We ourselves must proceed phenomenologically, that is to say, hermeneutically: these are the modes of being (*modi essendi*) that are expressed in modes of understanding (*modi intelligendi*), and in this way it can be discovered what there is in common in the approach of thought and in the structure of the universes reached in both cases, in the series of events, and in the postulates that are clearly stated. Perhaps this research is only a venture, but where can it be attempted if not at Eranos? It requires recourses other than those that suffice for philological discussions, means other than a transposition of methods or results ranging from historical criticism to criticism of the Qur'ān, which, at best, leads to nothing but a Qur'ān that has never been read by any believer. Our point of departure is a spiritual *fact*, a phenomenon of *understanding*: how has certain information common to the Bible and the Qur'ān been read and understood by spiritual individuals who had *faith* in these Books, and how is a certain type of common comprehension revealed in the manner of perceiving the hidden meaning of events and the universes that this meaning presupposes? The issue, then, is a comparative study that consists essentially in the hermeneutics of the "phenomenon of the Sacred Book."

I. Swedenborg's Spiritual Hermeneutics

1. The Theory of Correspondences

Swedenborgian hermeneutics[5] are governed by a general doctrine of correspondences, which is itself linked to a gnoseology [philosophy of cognition] that places at the highest degree of cognition an immediate spiritual perception, to which we can relate our term *hierognosis*. This cognition was the privilege of a very ancient humanity, the first humanity, the idea of which is fundamental in the work of Swedenborg. The state of these ancient peoples was still that of a celestial humanity, which means that in observing every possible object in the world and on the surface of the earth, they saw them, certainly, but they thought, by means of them, of the celestial and divine things that these objects represented or signified for them. Their visual (optic) perception was only a means. For them the process was as it is for our hearing when we listen to a speaker; we hear the words, of course, but actually it is not the words that we hear, it is their meanings. The decline began among the descendants of these celestial human beings when the object of sensory perception became the principal thing, instead of being the *instrument*. While for the first humanity, the objects of sensory cognition possessed a character that conformed them and subordinated them to their "internal man," to the extent that outside of this they had no interest in sensory things, their descendants, on the other hand, by placing the latter before those of the internal man, separated one from the other. In fact, they began to reason about spiritual things in the same manner as they reasoned about sensory things, and in this way they became spiritually blind.[6]

As Swedenborg repeats frequently in the course of his immense work, this is the reason that so few people know what "representations" and "correspondences" are. In order to know, it is necessary, in fact, to know that there is a spiritual world distinct from the natural world, and that the things which are diffused throughout the natural world from the spiritual world are representations of spiritual things. They are given this name because they "represent" the latter, and they represent them because they correspond to them,[7] that is, they *symbolize with* them. A very succinct idea of this is provided by the fact that our internal affections, everything that occurs in our thought and in our will, are manifested in the expressions of our face and look; the features of the face are their correspondences, the looks are their representations. The same holds true for gestures carried out by the body, actions produced by the muscles. Gestures and actions are representations of things that are in the soul; insofar as they agree, they are their correspondences.[8] But, of course, the mode of existence of these physiognomic images, these gestures and actions of the body, is not the same as that of the thoughts they express; they are natural things "representing" spiritual things. It may be said that the things belonging to the *internal person* are extended into images ("imaginalized") in the *external person*; thus, the things that appear in the external man are *representatives* of the internal man, and the things that agree between them form *correspondences*.[9]

The bipartition of the world, therefore, should be understood not only in the universal sense, according to which there is, on one hand, a Spiritual World (itself comprising the heavenly angelic world, the intermediate world of spirits, and the infernal world) and, on the other hand, a natural world where we live in the present life; it must also be understood that this bipartition applies to every human individual, in the sense that for each person his "internal person" is a spiritual world while his external being is for him a natural world.[10] In support of this bipartition, there is value in the principles of a cosmology for which natural forms are essentially effects; they cannot be seen as causes, still less as causes of causes, that is, sufficient to account by themselves for their appearances and mutations. Every form derives from the precise cause that it manifests and represents, and for this reason it is preceded by that cause.The same holds true for the various degrees of the spiritual world. This, too, is a point on which Swedenborg is in profound accord with every theosophy that is closely or distantly related to Neoplatonism,[11] but his conclusion is also based primarily on direct experience.

We know how far he extended his studies of anatomy, for example. That a man could, in addition, thanks to angelic assistance of which he was conscious, decipher in transparency the secrets of the invisible spiritual organism on an anatomical plate was an extraordinary privilege that Swedenborg never regarded as a result of personal merit, but as a pure divine favor. It was in this way that he knew, from direct experience, that in the three kingdoms of the natural world there is not the smallest thing that does not represent something in the spiritual world, and that does not have something in the spiritual world to which it corresponds. This is the secret that he elaborated on throughout his commentaries on the Bible, and this is the key to those *Arcana* that open most often onto an unforeseen horizon.[12] The more unforeseen because, while he lives in the body, man is capable of feeling and perceiving only a little of all this; we apply to celestial and spiritual things a fatal naturalization that degrades them into natural things homogeneous to our "external man," and within us the "internal man" has lost sensation and perception of these things. "Blessed at that time is he who is in correspondence, that is, whose external man corresponds to his internal man."[13]

In the modern Western world, he himself was certainly one of those rare Elect and, indeed, to judge by his influence, one who opened the path to many others. He wrote that "the existence of such correspondence had become so familiar that it would be difficult to name anything else that would be more familiar." He knew by experience that our whole existence derives from the spiritual world,[14] that without this connection with the spiritual world, neither man nor any part of man could subsist for a moment. It was also granted him to understand which angelic communities are in particular relation with each part of the human body, and what their qualities are. Briefly, everything in the natural world, in general as well as in the most infinitesimal detail, including constellations, atmospheres, the entirety and the components of the animal, vegetable, and mineral kingdoms—all this is nothing more than a sort of "representative theater" of the spiritual world, where we can see things in their beauty if we know how to see them in the state of their Heaven.[15]

Let us point out that this conception of things agrees, even in its lexicon, with that professed by the theosophers of the Light in Islam (the *Ishrāqīyūn* of Sohravardī, Ibn 'Arabi, Ṣadrā Shīrāzī, etc.): sensory things are apparitional forms, the places of epiphany (*maẓāhir*, plural of *maẓhar*), the *theatrum* of suprasensory universes (whence the idea of *maẓharīya*, the epiphanic or theophanic function of images). Stated more precisely, this epiphanic relation is already established among the universes that precede, ontologically, the sensory world. Thus, in the intermediate World of Spirits, which, according to Swedenborgian topography, is situated below the angelic worlds, there exist what are designated in his lexicon as continuous and innumerable "representatives" (or symbolic forms), which are the forms of spiritual and celestial things, not unlike those that are in this world, which abound as a result of the ideas, reflections, and conversations of the angels of the higher universes. For every angelic idea contains infinite things, in comparison with the idea of a spirit, and unless this idea were formed and shown "representatively" in an image corresponding to the level of spirits, or more precisely to the lower Sphere where there is a corresponding society of spirits, the latter would have difficulty understanding its content. These "representative" or symbolic forms may constitute long series, and the visionary theosopher to whom it was granted to be their witness could only estimate their length in quantities of earthly time, but he knew that it required pages and pages to describe them: they could present cities, palaces of astounding architectural artistry never seen, landscapes crossed by cavalcades of supernatural horsemen. It is also by means of these visions that humans who have become spirits are initiated after death into the higher universes.[16]

From all this emerges the fundamental plan of the spiritual universes. There are three heavens arranged in a hierarchy of increasing interiority and purity: a lower heaven, a middle heaven, and a higher heaven.The first is a natural realm, the "abode" of good spirits; the second is the abode of angelic spirits or spiritual angels; the third is the abode of the "celestial" angels (the term *celestial* here should by no means be confused with anything relating to astronomy, nor, in this context, especially with the *Angeli caelestes* of classical Avicennian cosmology). Just as there are three heavens, there are three senses in the Divine Word, the Bible: the natural sense, the spiritual sense, and the "celestial" sense. We will soon see that this is the basic doctrine of Swedenborgian hermeneutics. Each of these heavens is differentiated into innumerable communities; each of these, in turn, into innumerable individuals who, through their harmony, constitute, as it were, a person, and all of these communities together form a single Person. The communities result spontaneously from affinities of intelligence and love, just as some are differentiated from others according to the differences of their love and their faith. These differences are so innumerable that even the most general cannot be listed. Each angel and each community are, respectively, an image of the universal heaven, something like a "small heaven."[17]

But though Heaven is spoken of as an "abode," this must be understood as an abode that is the *state* of the internal man. That is why the topography of the *Infernum*, situated opposite, presents a distribution of its "abodes" symmetrical to those of the "abodes" of Heaven, because the demons and infernal spirits, as well as the angels and spirits that inhabit Heaven, were all human beings in this life, and each person bears within himself his heaven as he bears within himself his hell. By this law of interiority it is necessary to understand that the phases of *time* and the places of *space* are interior *states* of man as well;[18] Swedenborg mentions this frequently, and it must always be remembered. With this *hierocosmology* that determines in a parallel manner the structure of the hermeneutics of the Bible, we are undoubtedly at the heart of the Swedenborgian vision of the world. But we can only note here, very briefly, a few indications regarding certain aspects that derive from it and that are of consequence to our purpose: there is a double light, a double heat, a double Imagination, and finally there is the theme of the *Homo maximus*, which is of fundamental importance.

There is a double light: the light of the world and the light of Heaven, which we will again call here "celestial" light, in order to avoid any confusion with that of the astronomical sky. The first of these proceeds from the visible sun, the second proceeds from the spiritual Sun. For us, the first is natural or external, that is, with regard to the things that appear to the external person, since we cannot apprehend anything except by means of things that exist in our solar world, and that take form there through light and darkness. Ideas of time and space, at least insofar as these constitute an irreversible succession and an external localization, without which we cannot think of anything, are related to the light of the world. But the second, the celestial light, is for the internal spiritual person; he is within this light itself.[19]

When one speaks of correspondences and representations, and of their source and foundation, the issue, then, is one of *correspondence* between the things that relate to the light of the world of the external man and the things that relate to the celestial light of the internal man, for everything that exists in the first is the *representation* of what exists in the second. In order to grasp this "representativity" (or this symbolic function) that natural things assume of their own accord by virtue of their spiritual and celestial correspondences, it is necessary to utilize a higher faculty so well implanted in us that it is the one we carry with us into the other life; it is designated as spiritual sensitivity, the senses of the spirit (*animus*), or as *interior imagination.* For after death (this is one of the essential points of Swedenborg's doctrines) we possess the fullness of the human form—in the spiritual state, to be sure, and of a subtle constitution. This higher faculty, then, is so deep-rooted in us, and we are so deep-rooted in it, that we do not have to learn to use it. We are placed immediately in it as soon as we are liberated from our physical organism. On the other hand, during our life we usually remain ignorant of this higher faculty. There is a continual influx of things from the spiritual world into natural things; the former manifest themselves "representatively," symbolically, in the latter, and we are unaware of anything, totally given up to the natural things that we have rendered silent.[20]

For the more we are immersed in the things of this world, the more the things that relate to the celestial light appear to us paradoxically like darkness and emptiness, though inversely all that appears only in the light of this world constitutes thick darkness for the angels.[21] Yet these two lights are, together, everything that comprises our intelligence while our present life passes. Our natural imagination consists solely of forms and ideas of things, marvelously varied and structured, which we have apprehended through our corporeal vision, but our interior imagination consists solely of forms and ideas of things, even more marvelously varied and structured, which we have received through the vision of the spirit, in the celestial light, for by means of influx from the spiritual world the inanimate things of this world become endowed with life.[22]

There is more. It is necessary to speak not only of a double light but also of a double heat. "The heat of heaven [proceeds] from the spiritual sun, which is the Lord, and the heat of the world from the sun thereof, which is the luminary seen by our physical eyes. The heat of heaven manifests itself to the internal person by spiritual loves and affections, whereas the heat of the world manifests itself to the external person by natural loves and affections. The former heat causes the life of the internal person, but the latter the life of the external person; for without love and affection man cannot live at all. Between these two heats also there are correspondences."[23] Spiritual light and heat have as their opposites the infernal darkness and cold inhabited by the infernal spirits, who breathe only hatred and violence, fury and negation, tending to the destruction of the universe, to the point that if their rage were not continually combatted and repelled by the beings of the spiritual world, the entire human race would perish, unconscious of the secret of its history.[24]

It may be said that the dominant idea here is that at the source of every natural principle, whether of psychology or cosmology, there is a spiritual principle. Light and heat are related, respectively, to intelligence and will, or again to wisdom and love. When Swedenborg speaks of intelligence and will, his vocabulary refers to something far more profound than the two "faculties" so named in the psychology of philosophers; for him the two words designate two essential components of an organism that is the spiritual organism of man. This is also the reason that to the eyes of angels the light appears like light, but there are intelligence and wisdom in it, because the light derives from both. Similarly, the heat is perceived by angelic sensitivity as heat, but there is love in it, because it derives from love. Love is therefore called spiritual heat and constitutes the heat of a person's life, just as intelligence is called spiritual light and constitutes the light of a person's life. From this fundamental correspondence all the rest is derived.[25]

From this derives, for example, the idea that Swedenborg offers us of the first, celestial humanity, discussed above. As we will see, the initial chapters of the book of Genesis relate the origin and decline of that humanity. Swedenborg was shown, by a divine influx that he could not describe,[26] the nature of the discourse of these first people while they lived in this world, a silent discourse regulated not by the breath of external respiration but by a pure internal respiration. It is necessary to refer to the description that Swedenborg gives of the "discourse" of spirits and angels. Among all of them, discourse is carried out by representations, for they manifest everything they think about through marvelous variations of light and shade, in a living manner, to both the interior and the exterior vision of the one to whom they are speaking, and they introduce it into him by means of appropriate changes in the state of the affections experienced.

Among the angels of the interior heaven (the "spiritual angels"), discourse is even more beautiful, more attractively representative and symbolic, but the ideas that are formed there "representatively," symbolically, cannot be expressed *by words.* Spiritual things that pertain to the True, that is, to the category of intelligence, are expressed there by modifications of the celestial light, resulting in an infinite and wonderful variety of affections experienced. Spiritual things that pertain to the Good, that is, to the category of love, are expressed there by variations of heat and celestial blazing, setting all sorts of new affections into motion. As for the discourse of the angels of "the most interior heaven" (the "celestial angels"), it is also representative, symbolic, but it cannot be either apprehended by us or expressed *by any idea.* Nevertheless, there is such an idea within man, if he is in celestial love, and after the separation from his material body, he comes into this love as though born into it, although during his life in the material body he could not apprehend anything of it as an idea—just as he can also come into one or another of the forms corresponding to a lesser kind of love, for in his essential being, without any possible subterfuge, man is such as is his love.[27]

Finally, the vast doctrine of correspondences that unfolds like a phenomenology of angelic consciousness, together with the hierarchy of degrees of perception and representation that it implies, is recapitulated, so to speak, in the great theme of the *Homo maximus,* a theme that I had occasion to discuss here at Eranos several years ago in its striking "correspondence" (the word is certainly apt here) with the idea of the "Temple of Light" (*Haykal nūrānī*) of the Imām in Isma'ili gnosis.[28] We alluded to it a few moments ago, but we must now learn what image it is appropriate that it should represent for us when, throughout his immense biblical commentaries, Swedenborg utters this word: *the Lord* (*Dominus*). The theme in fact conceals the mystery itself of the divine anthropomorphosis as eternal theophany "in heaven."

"It is a truth most deeply hidden from the world," writes Swedenborg, "(and yet nothing is better known in the other life, even to every spirit), that all the parts of the human body have a correspondence with such things as are in heaven, insomuch that there is not even the smallest particle in the body, which has not something spiritual and celestial corresponding to it, or, what is the same, which has not heavenly communities corresponding to it: for these communities exist according to all the kinds and species of spiritual and celestial things, and indeed in such an order, that they represent together one person, and this as to all things in general and particular thereof, both interior and exterior. Hence it is, that the universal heaven is also called the Grand Man [*Homo maximus*]; and hence it is, that it has so often been said that one society belongs to one province of the body, another to another, and so forth. The reason is, because the Lord is the only Man, and Heaven represents Him..."[29]

These last lines are amplified by many passages in the *Arcana Coelestia*. Let us only note here the postulate that they imply, which is in profound accord with all mystical theologies. In his personal vocabulary, Swedenborg differentiates an *Esse infinitum* and an *Existere infinitum*, the term *existere* here being practically the equivalent of *manifestation*.[30] Jehovah (let us not emphasize Swedenborg's fidelity to this vocalization of the sacred tetragrammaton) is the *Esse infinitum*. As such, He is not manifested to man and has no "influence" within man or upon man. He is the *deity* in His absolute *absconditum* (the *hyperousion* of Greek theology, He who, in Isma'ili theosophy, is the *Mobdi'*, the Principle, Super-Being). He cannot be manifested to man and act within or upon man except by means of the human Essence, that is, by an *existere divinum* in the essential human Form. The figure of this theophany or of this eternal anthropomorphosis is "the Lord"; thus all of Swedenborgian theosophy is dominated by this figure of the *Anthrōpos* (which brings to mind the visions of Enoch, the Ascension of Isaiah, etc.). Because the Divine cannot have any "influence" within man except by means of the human Essence of the "Lord," there is no conjunction possible with the "supreme divinity" or deity of the Lord, which remains transcendent to His epiphanic divinity "in heaven"; conjunction is possible only with His Divine Humanity, because an idea of His ***Humanum Divinum*** is possible, but no idea is possible of the Divine in Itself.[31] In other words, the "Lord" is the Divine Man who exists from all eternity; He is, certainly, Jehovah Himself, but Jehovah as He is an epiphany "in heaven," and as in this eternal theophany He assumes the Human so that men (and therefore angels, who constitute the higher celestial humanity) can have an idea about the Divinity.[32] There is thus identity, but an identity differentiated as to the revealed and the concealed (the *ẓāhir* and the *bāṭin*). For the secret of the Divine Manifestation, of the Theophany, is that the Lord appears to each in a form corresponding to the respective capacity of each. (This is exactly what Ibn 'Arabi teaches us in Islamic theosophy).[33] Swedenborg is explicit: the Lord does not conceal Himself, but the evil make it appear as though He concealed Himself, as though He had no existence.

It is this *Kyrios Anthrōpos* of whom it is said that He himself *is* heaven,[34] and this identification indeed agrees with the multiplicity of differentiated theophanies. In fact, insofar as heaven "represents" Him, the relationship of the Lord to heaven as *Homo maximus* is analogous to the relationship of our sun to our perceptible world. The Lord is the spiritual Sun, and by means of Him there is light in all that is intelligence and there is heat in all that is love.[35] But then, precisely as such, the Lord Himself *is also Homo maximus*; in the strict sense, in the kyriological sense, He Himself alone is *Man*, *Anthrōpos*, and all humans are called ***men*** in His name, from Him, because they are Images of Him,[36] to the extent that they are in Good, that is, in the affection of love. The following lines recapitulate it best: "The Grand Man [*Homo maximus*], relatively to man, is the universal heaven of the Lord; but the Grand Man, in the highest sense, is the Lord alone, for heaven is from Him, and all things therein correspond to Him.... Hence they who are in the heavens are said to be in the Lord, yea, in His body, for the Lord is the all of heaven."[37]

The theme of the *Homo maximus* is, therefore, the key to the monadological conception that makes a "little heaven" of every individual angelic spirit, since the heaven to which he belongs and which is in him is *Homo maximus.* And it is there, in that immanence of the All in each and of each in the All, that the angelological anthropology postulated by the doctrine of correspondences culminates: "All spirits and angels," writes Swedenborg, "appear to themselves as people, of a similar face and body, with organs and members; and this for the reason that their Inmost conspires to such a form . . . . The universal heaven is such, that every one is as it were the center of all, for each is the center of influxes through the heavenly form from all, and hence an image of heaven results to everyone, and makes him like to itself, that is, a person; for such as the general is, such is a part of the general."[38]

We have tried to sketch out, in allusive lines, the doctrine of correspondences, respecting which Swedenborg states that, although it is unknown in our time, it was regarded by very ancient humanity, the initial celestial humanity, as a true science, indeed as the preeminent science, the science of sciences, and it was so universally known that men wrote all of their books at that time in the "language of correspondences." Similarly, their rituals and the ceremonies of their religion consisted solely of correspondences, and it is because they thought spiritually in this way about terrestrial things that they were in community with the angels of heaven.[39]

Before the Divine Word, the text of the Bible that we read today, there was another Word that is now lost. The books attributed to Moses and others refer to books that are lost today.[40] We will see the meaning that Swedenborg gives to the disappearance of Enoch, who, with the help of his people, had collected the correspondences of the language of this humanity; knowledge of it is supposed to have been transmitted to a posterity that includes almost all the peoples of Asia, from where it was transmitted to the Greeks, among whom it became mythology.[41] In any case, Swedenborg considers it a demonstrable certainty that before the Israelite Word, there existed on earth an ancient Word, particularly in Asia. He has shown, he says in his *Memorabilia*, that "this Word is preserved in heaven among the angels who lived in those times; and it survives at the present day among the nations of Great Tartary."[42] Whether this preciseness refers to Tibet or, as is now thought, to Outer Mongolia,[43] can it refer to anything but the scriptures of Mahayana Buddhism? For Swedenborg's heaven, as well as his vision of hierohistory, are vast enough to contain all religions.

2. *Principles of Spiritual Hermeneutics*

As was said above, the doctrine of correspondences—the fundamental law of analogy that permits positing a plurality of universes among which there is a symbolic relationship—controls Swedenborgian hermeneutics and determines its principles and application. It is still more precise to say that this doctrine *is* this hermeneutics itself; or, again, what is expressed in this hermeneutics as a mode of understanding (*modus intelligendi*) is the mode of being itself (*modus essendi*) that is experienced and that proclaims itself as the being in correspondence of an entire aggregate of levels of being, "representative" of one another, "signifying" one another. There is no question, therefore, of bringing these correspondences "from outside" and then relating them to the text of the Bible; they *are* that which the text of the Bible signifies, the Word in the act of being understood in the true sense, that is, in the spiritual sense.

Thus, the guiding principles of Swedenborgian hermeneutics, that is, the general principles that will regulate the application of exegesis of the details of the texts, relate, on one hand, to the aspects under which the biblical text appears, the *styles* of the Word, as Swedenborg calls them, and, on the other, to the hierarchical structure of the universes to which these styles correspond. The first consideration is concerned with determining what the historical sense is and how it relates to the spiritual sense and with preventing any confusion of the latter with the allegorical sense. Once this differentiation is established, the use of the spiritual sense in its plurality will be accomplished in accordance with the schema of the three heavens, described above.

For Swedenborgian hermeneutics, the entirety of the biblical text, the Word, appears as though written in *four* different styles.[44] The differentiation of these styles forces us to anticipate the theme of the succession of the ages of humanity, and to note, from this point on, that in the Swedenborgian vocabulary the word *Ecclesia* (assembly) takes on a meaning so broad that the "spiritual assembly" includes the angelic universes and the World of Spirits, as well as the different ages of earthly humanity and of the humanity of other universes (to prevent any misunderstanding, it should also be said that for Swedenborg knowledge of these extraterrestrial humanities does not relate in any way to a physical humanity of the sort that might be encountered by the astronauts of our spaceships, but a humanity perceived in the spiritual state while the visionary was "in the Spirit," a perception which implies that a *threshold* was crossed, one that is normally crossed only after death). Briefly, the Swedenborgian concept goes so far beyond the usual connotation of the word *church* that it seems preferable to avoid any misapprehension and retain the Latin term *Ecclesia*, giving it a particular meaning for this essay.

Of the four biblical styles, the first is a style that, under a historical form, in fact presents a *symbolic history*; the first eleven chapters of the book of Genesis are such a history. The second is the historical style in the strict sense of the word, that of the historical books of the Bible. The third is the prophetic style.[45] The fourth is the style of the Psalms, intermediate between the prophetic style and that of ordinary speech. It is necessary here only to emphasize the problems posed by the first two.

The first of the styles of the Word was that of celestial humanity, described above, which constituted what Swedenborg designates as the Most Ancient Assembly, the *Antiquissima Ecclesia*.

The circumstances, the mode of being and knowing of the people of this *Ecclesia,* differed essentially from the status of modern humanity in our time. We already know that they regarded all corporeal things, which, in a general way, are the object of sensory perception, as dead things if they are perceived separately from what they represent. Their mode of knowing, the fundamental state of their consciousness, was characterized by an immediate perception of spiritual and celestial things that sensory earthly things represent. Therefore, their characteristic mode of expression was that of men for whom the perception of objects is immediately transmuted into a perception of spiritual things, thus transmuting inanimate things into living things.[46] They saw, certainly, with their eyes or perceived by means of their other senses everything that is the object of sensory perception, but simultaneously and immediately they perceived things of another order, "represented," symbolized, by sensory things.

It is this which leads Swedenborg to a detailed analysis of the first of the biblical styles, the one in which the first chapters of Genesis, up to the story of Abraham, are written.[47] These chapters are not history in the strict sense of the word; nor are they what, in our time, is called myth or a mythic tale. The form of a *continuum*, of a succession of events, was spontaneously given by these men to spiritual things whose *representation* they perceived in sensory things, imbuing those things with life. We thus grasp the process that, previous to any external, material, historical datum, permits the appearance of something like a "history," the mental operation in which is found to be, in the final analysis, the secret of the *historicization* of every history, whatever it may be. In other words, all historicity, in order to be constituted as such, presumes a *metahistorical* factor. Here begins the transition to the historical style in the strict sense of the word. But since establishing the legitimacy of spiritual hermeneutics is the question under discussion here, an observation must be made. Because the historical style in the strict sense of the word will originate from the symbolic or metahistorical style of the *Antiquissima Ecclesia*, the historical parts of the Bible are equally representative and contain a spiritual sense—indeed, several spiritual senses. In addition, the manner in which Swedenborg analyzes the gnoseology of the first celestial humanity (and he returns to this subject on many occasions), the mode of spontaneous perception of the suprasensory in the sensory, indicates very well that it is not for a moment permitted to confuse this spiritual sense with allegory. Allegories are invented after the fact, they serve to transpose what was already knowable otherwise, to disguise previously existing images or thoughts. Now, the "first biblical style," that of the first eleven chapters of Genesis, is the only manner of expressing a spiritual perception of origins, an unconditional perception, previous to all explanation, but itself giving origin to perhaps inexhaustible explanations: the *arcana* of it are, in fact, innumerable.

The second style is the historical style in the strict sense of the word, which is found in the "books of Moses" beginning with the stories concerning the epoch of Abraham and in the books of Joshua, Judges, Samuel, and Kings. In these books, the historical facts are indeed such as they appear according to the literal sense; however, they all contain, at the same time in general and in their particulars, completely different things according to the internal sense.[48] This is true because these historical facts are themselves *representatives*; all the words that express them are *significatives*, that is, beneath the appearance of external things they signify internal things; beneath the appearance of earthly things and events, spiritual or celestial things and events. This is so for all the books of the Bible called "historical." Their content appears to be history pure and simple in the literal sense, no doubt; but in the internal sense they conceal innumerable *arcana coelestia*, which cannot be seen while the eyes of thought remain fixed on the materiality of external historical facts. The Divine Word is like a body concealing a living soul. But this soul remains unrevealed; it is even difficult to believe that there is a soul there, the being that survives death, before the thought withdraws from corporeal things in order to reach the things of the soul. A new birth is necessary. Just as the physical body of man must die in order that the human being may find himself and see himself in the spiritual world and communicate with spiritual beings, so spiritual things, the internal sense, remain absolutely invisible until the corporeal things, the external data of the literal sense, are as though dead. The natural *vessels* are one thing, the spiritual things that they contain are another.[49]

If this is true, if the "historical style" of the Bible conceals so many *arcana*, it is because the men of the *Antiqua Ecclesia*, those of the period designated by the name of Noah, gathered in the form of doctrines (*doctrinalia*) the things that the men of antediluvian humanity, those of the *Antiquissima Ecclesia*, had *signified* in perceiving them by a direct spiritual apprehension. It is necessary to be attentive here to the precision of Swedenborgian vocabulary. For the men of postdiluvian humanity, these same things became *significatives*, that is, they led them to discover internal things and, by means of these, to discover spiritual things and then celestial things. But it happened that this symbolic knowledge itself declined; earthly things themselves began to be regarded as sacred, without a thought about their signification. These earthly things thus became pure *representatives*; with them was born the *Ecclesia repraesentativa*, at the beginning of the period of Abraham. These *representatives*, therefore, have their origin in the *significatives* of the *Antiqua Ecclesia*, and those in turn have their origin in the celestial ideas of the *Antiquissima Ecclesia*.[50]

The situation reverts here to the one we described at the beginning (see prologue) as typified in the Arabic term *ḥikāyat*. The disciple of Swedenborg knows what effort will be demanded of him: an effort whose success depends upon conditions other than human cleverness or good will, upon a regeneration, a new birth that is birth in the spiritual world. A new *modus intelligendi* would be impossible without a new *modus essendi* (the idea of esoteric hermeneutics as being like a spiritual birth, *wilādat rūhānīya*, is also present in Shi'ism and Isma'ilism). The soul and the life of the Word are in the internal sense, and the soul that is life is not manifested until the literal sense has, in fact, seemed to vanish. In short, it is necessary to learn to read the Word as the angels read it, or, more precisely, according to the terms that Swedenborg uses in relating his unique experience of "events in heaven"; it is necessary to read the Divine Word as the angels perceive it when it is being read by someone in this world.[51]

The angels

> know nothing at all of what is in the letter, not even the proximate meaning of a single word; still less do they know the names of the countries, cities, rivers, and persons that occur so frequently in the historical and prophetical parts of the Word. They have an idea only of the things signified by the words and the names. Thus by Adam in paradise they perceive the *Antiquissima Ecclesia*, yet not that *Ecclesia*, but the faith in the Lord of that *Ecclesia*. By Noah they perceive the *Ecclesia* (spiritual assembly) that remained with the descendants of the *Antiquissima Ecclesia* and that continued to the time of Abram. By Abraham they by no means perceive that individual, but a saving faith, which he represented; and so on. Thus they perceive spiritual and celestial things entirely apart from the words and the names.[52]

What they read are the *arcana* contained in each individual verse and whose multiplicity would astound us, if we had any idea of it, for their amplification is multiplied from heaven to heaven. All the words of the letter are represented in a lively and dazzling manner in the world of the angelic spirits, which is a world constituted of "representative ideas," of which are made the opening of those *apparentiae reales* that are the corresponding celestial landscapes. In turn, these ideas are perceived by the spiritual angels of the second heaven, then by the celestial angels of the third heaven, each time with an abundance, plenitude, and magnificence whose growth is limitless.[53]

That is why, whether it is a matter of the content of spiritual perceptions typified or "historicized" in symbolic histories, or whether it is a matter of historical tales in the strict sense of the word, that is, of historical events having taken place just as they are described, in fact the hermeneutic imperative is the same, for the real external events, the words that describe them, contain *arcana coelestia* exactly like the typifications in symbolic histories. This may appear strange, for at first sight, where there is a historical account, the thought remains fixed on the letter and does not suppose that something else may be signified. Yet without this other sense, the internal sense, "how would a historical account in the Word differ from a history told by a profane historian?" And then of what use would it be to know the age of Noah, the month and the day when the flood began, if it did not involve something else entirely other than history, namely, an *arcanum coeleste*? Who cannot see that this saying, "All the fountains of the great deep were broken up, and the cataracts of heaven were opened," constitutes, in fact, *prophetic* words.[54]

These details concerning the different styles of the Word underpin the entire use of the hermeneutics. As we have already learned,[55] just as there are three heavens—highest heaven, middle heaven, and lower heaven—so there are, corresponding respectively to each of these kingdoms or abodes, three senses in the divine Word: a "celestial" sense, a spiritual sense, and a natural sense. This triad corresponds to a general structure that Swedenborg explains in detail. When it is stated that the literal sense of the Word is the basis, the covering or the veil, the support of its spiritual sense and its celestial sense, it is because in everything divine there are three things: a first thing, an intermediate thing, and a last thing. That which is first proceeds through the intermediate toward what is last, and thus takes on existence and subsistence. The first is, therefore, in the intermediate and is also, by that means, in what is last. In this connection, what is last is that which contains; at the same time it is the basis, and thus it turns out to be the support. These three things may be designated, respectively, as the end, the cause, and the effect; or as the being that is the end, the becoming that is the cause, and the manifestation that is the effect. Everything in the world, insofar as it is complete, is so constituted by a triad,[56] and this is also the structure of the Divine Word. In its literal or natural sense an internal or spiritual sense is hidden, and within that a sense still more internal, an inmost (*intimus*) and celestial sense. "Thus the lowest sense, which is the natural, and called the sense of the letter, is the containant of the two internal senses, and consequently their basis and support."[57]

At this point we can move forward to the solution of the apparent paradox of spiritual hermeneutics. The two higher senses, spiritual and celestial, are found together simultaneously *within* the literal sense. To understand the process of this triadic structure, it is necessary to consider with Swedenborg that "in heaven" and in the world the order of things is according to a double type:[58] there is a *successive* order, a mode of structure where one thing succeeds and follows after another, from the highest to the lowest; and there is a *simultaneous* order, where things are juxtaposed, from the inmost to the outermost, as in going from the common center to the periphery of several concentric circles.

Successive order may be considered to be like sections of the column of a temple, where the circumference increases in volume from the summit to the base. In the order of *succession*, what is at the summit and first in origin corresponds to what is interior and central in the order of *simultaneity*. So that we may have a representation of this, let us imagine with Swedenborg that this column, which serves here as a term of comparison, descends and sinks down upon itself to form a plane surface, its summit—that is, its origin in the *successive* order—now occupying the center of the new figure in the *simultaneous* order. It is the same in the case of the Divine Word. The celestial, the spiritual, and the natural proceed in *successive* order and finally they appear *simultaneously* in the text that is at our disposal: the celestial sense and the spiritual sense are there together, dwelling concealed in the literal sense. The latter is the containant, the basis, and the protection to such a degree that in the absence of this natural literal sense, the celestial sense and the spiritual sense would not be the Word, but would be like spirit and life without a body, or like a temple with many sanctuaries and a Holy of Holies at its center, but lacking a roof and walls, so that the temple would be exposed to the depredations of thieves and wild beasts.[59]

The apparent paradox of spiritual hermeneutics thus turns out to be resolved. On one hand, we are told that it is necessary to learn to read the Word as the angelic spirits read it, and for this it is necessary to pass through a spiritual birth that is accompanied by the *death* of the natural literal sense. On the other hand, this natural sense is shown to us as being the state of Manifestation, to which the proceeding of the Divine Word leads and in which it ends; it forms the covering, the basis, and the protection of the latter, the body indispensable to the spirit and the life. No misunderstanding is possible, however. We are faced with the same imperative as that which is posed to the esoteric hermeneutics of Shi'ism in general: the simultaneity and the necessity of maintaining the simultaneity of the spiritual sense and the literal appearance, of the exoteric (*ẓāhir*) and the esoteric (*bāṭin*). The situation is, in fact: either this simultaneity is not noticed by the profane, in which case the natural sense forms a protective wall against any violation of the sanctuary; or else it is known to the spiritual adept, but in this knowledge itself a transmutation of the natural sense occurs, the covering becoming transparent, diaphanous. Every natural thing tends to its *Geistleiblichkeit*, to that state of "spiritual body," which Oetinger, as a faithful disciple of Swedenborg, made into a fundamental idea, because it is also the state of beings and things observed by Swedenborg in the course of visionary states reported in the *Memorabilia* or the *Diarium Spirituale*.

Hence the double warning against the possible double profanation. On one hand, there is a profanation of the natural literal sense, if this is diverted from its end, explained as though it were sufficient unto itself and in that way desacralized, deprived of its internal and external sacredness. On the other hand, there is also always the danger, on the part of man, of a corruption of the spiritual sense. This spiritual sense is that of the Divine Humanity, the sense in which the angels of heaven *are*, but which no one can see, says Swedenborg, without being placed by the Lord in divine truths. If man wants to attain to it simply by means of a few correspondences known by him theoretically, heaven closes itself to him and he is in peril of falling into a state of spiritual insanity. It is for this reason that guards were posted before the sanctuary of the Divine Word, in which they are called *Cherubim*.[60] And by this word, our attention is drawn to the drama that consists in the succession of the ages of humanity, its *true* history, its spiritual history.

3. The Ages of Humanity

This history would be nothing more than the continued decline of the internal person, if there were not, from period to period, a "Judgment in Heaven" that effected a reestablishment. Swedenborgian theosophy distinguishes four great periods (themselves comprising subdivisions).[61] We have already acquainted ourselves with the first, designated as the Most Ancient (or primal) Assembly, the *Antiquissima Ecclesia*. This is the period of a very ancient humanity during which heaven acted in unison with man, because, contrary to what was to occur afterward, it was through direct influence upon the *internal person* and by means of it that heaven influenced the external person. Consequently, humanity not only had enlightenment and immediate spiritual perception but, by means of direct relations with the angels, was also informed of heavenly things and of everything that concerns eternal life.

We already know that because they were "internal people," their sensory perception of external things was simultaneously the perception of something divine and heavenly. They perceived at the same time, for example, the dawn and what it had in common with the glory of the spirits' love for the world, as well as why it is that the Lord is called the morning, the *East*, dawn, daybreak. Similarly, the man of this *Ecclesia* was not only compared to a tree, he *was* himself a tree, a garden, that is, a paradise. For it was the same general affective tonality that modulated all perceptions, those of the senses as well as those of the intellect; therefore, everything that these humans saw with their eyes was the same as heavenly things, living things, and their worship was able to be a worship that was purely internal.[62] Even their physiology was different, since their organism possessed that silent internal respiration of which not a trace remained in the humanity that was drowned in the flood, nor in the humanity that succeeded it.[63] Briefly, it is this epoch that is designated as the *Golden Age*. Good, in fact, has a double origin corresponding to the two constituent organs of the spiritual organism: in the will, where it is love, and in the intelligence, where it is wisdom and truth. Humans, then, were at once in the fundamental form of the good that corresponds to the most interior heaven, that of the celestial angels. *Gold* is the symbol of this good which is celestial love, and it is this golden age that the Word describes as paradise.

However, in the generations that successively formed the posterity of this blissful humanity, communication with heaven was progressively lost. Things reached the point that, in the humanity that was obliged to pass through the spiritual catastrophe called the Flood, there was no longer perception of anything else in external objects except what is of this world, material and terrestrial. On the other hand, communication of man with his hell was opened, and it is this hell that became the general affective tonality of all perceptions, to the point at which there was no longer any desire to know that something spiritual and celestial exists.

The episode of the disappearance of Enoch or of his taking by God is placed here, a disappearance that signifies the preservation of *doctrinalia* before permitting the raising up of a new postdiluvian spiritual humanity, that of the *Antiqua Ecclesia*, which succeeded the *Antiquissima*. However, because this humanity was no longer a celestial humanity, but only a spiritual humanity, it knew, certainly, but no longer had the direct perception of what was thenceforth enveloped for it in symbols (the *repraesentativa* and the *significativa*) derived from the celestial perceptions of the first people.[64] There was no longer any perception, for example, of the dawn as the Lord, but there was a knowledge of what the dawn signified and symbolized. There was no longer a direct influx from heaven into humanity, but there was an influx by means of correspondences and representations that are the external forms of heavenly things (their *ḥikāyat*, the things that *imitate* them and that are their "history"). The transition to analogical knowledge, to the perception of symbols, comes about as a derivation of direct spiritual perception, of hierognosis. The time of the *Antiqua Ecclesia* is designated as the *Silver Age*, because men are no longer in the fundamental form of good, which is celestial love—where love is itself knowledge. The influx of heaven opens in them in the good of intelligence, which is wisdom. Silver is the symbol of this spiritual good, which is essentially truth, as gold is the symbol of celestial good, which is essentially love.

When the knowledge of correspondences and *repraesentativa* degenerated into magic, though, this *Antiqua Ecclesia* perished in its turn; a third *Ecclesia* succeeded it, in which worship was entirely inspired by similar observations, but their signification was not known.[65] This *Ecclesia* was instituted with the Israelite and Jewish nation. But because knowledge of celestial things and those relating to eternal life could not be imparted to it by an influx into the internal man, the angels of heaven would sometimes converse with certain men, the elite of this *Ecclesia judaica*, so that all the others could be instructed by them concerning external things, for lack of being instructed regarding internal things. Because these people were in natural good, they received with respect what was taught to them in this way. This time was called the *Age of Bronze*, because bronze symbolizes this form of natural good, which is in the same relationship to the preceding two as is the natural literal sense to the spiritual sense and the celestial sense.

Finally, even natural good no longer continued to exist in the people of the *Ecclesia*. At this point the Event occurred that cannot be understood in the Swedenborgian perspective except by mobilizing around it all the great guiding themes of his theosophical theology. Let us only say here that, Paulinism having been set aside, that is, in the case of a Christian theology such as that of Swedenborg, which takes great care to avoid any confusion between evangelical theology and Pauline theology,[66] the meaning of the Divine Incarnation on earth as well as its relationship to an eternal divine anthropomorphosis are profoundly different from the theological teachings of the official churches. Among other things, the meaning of the Incarnation has nothing to do with the idea of a redemption, a compensation, and "atonement"; it is essentially a combat or, rather, the continuation of a combat begun at the beginning of the ages. In addition, although He assumed the terrestrial human form only once in person, the Lord "came" each time an *Ecclesia* was devastated.[67] This "coming" of the Lord is the triumph that breaks the infernal assault which threatens to invade the World of Spirits, and it is the possibility given once more to man to receive from Him the influx of heaven and thereby to become enlightened.

A fourth *Ecclesia* was then constituted, the *Ecclesia christiana*. In that *Ecclesia* all knowledge regarding heavenly things and eternal life proceeds uniquely from the Divine Word, by means of which man receives influx and light, since it was written in correspondences and representative images that signify and symbolize heavenly things. The angels of heaven come into these heavenly things when someone reads the Word, that is, the Bible, and when his internal vision opens to these internal things. Thus, from that time on, by means of the Word, conjunction is effected with each person to the degree to which that person *is* in the good that *is* love. Unfortunately, because the men of the *Ecclesia christiana* extinguished this flame, divine influx does not open among them except in partial and abstract truths, without any connection with the form of good, which is love. That is why this time is called the *Age of Iron.*[68]

The spiritual history of humanity therefore constitutes a drama in several acts, and the intermission between these acts causes the appearance of a characteristic conception that overturns completely the usual concept of "Last Judgment," a concept that the theology of our day, in its powerlessness, includes among those "myths" that are necessary to "demythologize." Swedenborg speaks neither of "myth" nor of "demythologizing." The Last Judgment signifies the last times of an *Ecclesia*, and it is also the final state in the life of each person, for every person's resurrection follows his exit from this world. Each *Ecclesia* is terminated by a Last Judgment, and we have just read that the Lord "comes" each time there is a Last Judgment, that is, the transition from an old *Ecclesia* to a new one. Here, the Swedenborgian idea of Judgment converges in a remarkable manner with the Isma'ili idea of *Qiyāmat* (judgment and resurrection), ending a period and marking the transition to a new period in the cycle of prophecy (from the period of Adam to that of Noah, from the period of Noah to that of Abraham, etc., from the period of Jesus to that of Muḥammad). There was a Last Judgment of the *Antiquissima Ecclesia* (called Adamic) when its posterity perished; it is that destruction (always in the spiritual sense) which is described as the Flood. There was a Last Judgment of the *Antiqua Ecclesia* (called Noachian) when almost all had succumbed to magic or idolatry. There was a Last Judgment of the *Ecclesia repraesentativa* when the ten tribes were taken into captivity and later during the dispersion. As to the Last Judgment of the *Ecclesia christiana*, it is signified in the vision of the Apocalypse as "a new heaven and a new earth," that is, in the vision of the New Jerusalem, *Nova Hierosolyma*.[69]

The internal sense of this vision has been so generally unknown that when the Last Judgment is mentioned, everyone imagines an event that must be accompanied by the destruction of the world, by a physical catastrophe embracing our terrestrial globe and bringing an end to the visible world, and only then "the dead shall be raised" to be brought to judgment. But all those who accept such conjectures completely ignore the fact that the internal sense of these prophetic statements (those of the Apocalypse, as well as those of the Gospel of Matthew)[70] is a sense that is totally different from the appearances of the literal sense: the "heaven" does not signify the astronomical sky, the "earth" does not signify the telluric mass of our planet, but does signify that *Ecclesia* which is the spiritual world,[71] and it is in the spiritual world that the Judgment has been pronounced henceforth on our *Age of Iron*.[72] Certainly, the vision of the kings of the earth making war on the horseman mounted on the white horse, who appeared when heaven opened (Rev. 19:11 ff.), and that of the dragon pursuing into the wilderness the woman who had brought forth a man-child (Rev. 12), indicate that much time will be needed for the spiritual sense to be recognized and for there to be a response to the call of the angel standing in the sun, gathering all the fowls that fly in the midst of heaven to the supper of the great God (Rev. 19:17).[73]

It was just said that "much time will be needed." But basically what does this expression mean? What does "the succession of time" mean, when the the question is one of an essentially spiritual history? Repeatedly in his enormous work Swedenborg reminds us that the ideas of succession of time and localization in an external space relate only to our sensory world; in the suprasensory world everything consists essentially and uniquely of changes and modifications of spiritual states, which may well appear as something like time and space, yet the angels do not have the least idea of what we call time and space.[74] It is the real state of each person that determines, in the other world, *his* time and *his* space; thus, time becomes reversible, spatial distances vary according to intensity of desire. This must never be forgotten, in order not to be astonished at scenes that Swedenborg, in the course of his "visions in the Spirit," witnessed in that other world where reality *is* vision and vision *is* reality. It must also not be forgotten when it is a matter of understanding the *sense* of the spiritual history that we have sketched since the *Antiquissima Ecclesia*, and that is entirely different from what is called in our time the "sense of history." It is completely different because the verb can always be put *in the present tense*; it is a history that is always imminent, whose sense is, consequently, eminently *current*, *present*. In just this way celestial humanity, from its origin, was not, *is* not itself anything other than the *seventh* day of Creation. It is the six days of Creation, the *hexaēmeron*, that constitute the key to this history and that give it its present sense, because what they measure is not a more or less mythical cosmogony, but is the creation, the raising up, of the *spiritual man*. And it is with this teaching that the immense work of the *Arcana Coelestia* opens.

4. *The Hexaēmeron of the Creation of Spiritual Man*

How should the first two chapters of the book of Genesis be understood in their internal, that is, spiritual, sense? It must be done by applying what the Christian world has so utterly forgotten: that everything in the Word, to the smallest detail, envelops and signifies spiritual and celestial things. If this is ignored, life itself withdraws from the dead letter, as the external man dies when he is separated from the internal man. In the absence of this, what else is there to discover in the sense of the letter except that the subjects treated are cosmogony, the creation of the world, the Garden of Eden that is called Paradise, and Adam as the first man created? Who would imagine anything else? And yet, in fact, the first chapter of the book of Genesis in its internal sense treats of the new creation of man, his new birth, that is, his *spiritual regeneration*, and thus of the establishment of the *Antiquissima Ecclesia*.[75]

Now, the times, that is, the *states*, of the spiritual regeneration of man are divided into six and are called the "six days" or periods of his creation (the *hexaēmeron*); they proceed from the moment when there is still nothing of a man, to when there is something of a man, and end by reaching the "sixth day," when he becomes *Imago Dei*.[76] Analyzed more closely, the succession of these six days or periods beginning with "prehumanity" is presented as follows: the *first day* is the state of childhood, followed by the state that immediately precedes regeneration; this is a state of "emptiness," or "thick darkness." The *second day* or second state is when the distinction is made between things that belong to the *internal man* and those that belong to the *external man*, in other words, those that belong to the Lord and those that are characteristic of man. The *third day* is that of internal change (conversion, *metanoia*), henceforth it is the internal man that acts, but his works are still *inanimate* things, because he thinks that they come from himself. The *fourth day* is the state of man affected by love and enlightened by faith, that is, by the "two lights" that are within him. But it is only on the *fifth day* that he speaks by faith and that the works produced by him are "animated"; they are called "fish of the sea" and "birds of the sky."

Finally, the *sixth day*: the spiritual man, who, by means of faith and love simultaneously, acts according to and expresses what is true and good. The works that he produces are thenceforth called a "living soul," and he himself is *Imago Dei*. Nevertheless, his natural life still finds its pleasure and its support in things that belong to the body and the senses; thus, a combat persists until the work of the sixth day attains its completion in the *seventh*, when under the sway of pure love man becomes celestial. In our time, however, most people do not go beyond the first state; a few achieve the second state; others, the third, fourth, and fifth; a few, the sixth; scarcely any achieve the seventh state.[77]

What emerges immediately is the distinction made between the spiritual man (the sixth day) and the celestial man (the seventh day). This differentiation corresponds to the hierarchy of the Swedenborgian heaven, and it may be said that the "seven days" characterize in their way the degrees of Swedenborgian initiation and spiritual hierarchy. But Swedenborg deplores the fact that in our time, "none have been acquainted with the nature of the celestial man, and few with that of the spiritual man, whom in consequence of this ignorance they have considered to be the same as the celestial man, notwithstanding the great difference that exists between them."[78]

What is this difference, characterized as the transition from the sixth day to the seventh day? It is said of the spiritual man that he is *Imago Dei*; but the image is *according to the likeness* of the model, it is not *the* likeness itself, the similitude. The spiritual man is an image; he is called a "son of light" (John 12:35-36), a "friend" (John 15:14-15). The celestial man *is* the likeness itself, the similitude; he is called a "son of God" (John 1:12-13).[79] So long as man is spiritual (the sixth day), his dominion proceeds from the external man to the internal. But when he becomes celestial (the seventh day), his dominion proceeds from the internal man to the external, because his activity proceeds from pure love.[80]

Stated clearly in the commentary on the first two chapters of Genesis is the fundamental idea of Swedenborgian anthropology, dominated by the two categories of intelligence and will: things relating to the cognitions of faith are called spiritual; all those that are of love for the Lord and the neighbor are called celestial; the former belong to man's intelligence, the latter to his will.[81] With regard to the differentiation that is under discussion, we have then: the spiritual man (the sixth day) is he in whom predominate the faith and wisdom that belong to the intelligence; this is the *Imago Dei.* The celestial man (the seventh day) is he in whom predominates love, which belongs to the will, and this primacy of love is *the* divine likeness or similitude.[82] Herein lies the profound meaning of the verse: "Male and female created He them" (Gen. 1:27). The intelligence of the spiritual man, that is, all his power of understanding, is what the men of the *Antiquissima Ecclesia* called the *male*; will, that is, the fundamental power of love, which is the heart, the *nucleus* of the human being, is what they called the *female.* The conjunction of the two was for them the archetype of the heavenly marriage.[83] The appearance of Eve will be understood, as we will see, on the basis of the same anthropology.

Thus, the entire schema of this anthropology appears in perfect symmetry with the doctrine of the three heavens, the three categories of beings who have their "abode" there, and the three senses of the Divine Word. The first chapter of the book of Genesis discusses the spiritual man; the second chapter discusses the celestial man; that man was formed from the dead man. (1) The dead man, that is, spiritually dead, does not recognize anything as true and good except that which belongs to the material body and to this world. The ends that influence him concern only the life of this world. Even if a suggestion is made to him regarding knowledge of another world, a suprasensory world, he refuses it; he cannot believe in it. If he must confront a combat in his soul, that is, in the combat for the soul, he is defeated in advance. He is the slave of his external servitudes: fear of the law, of the loss of life, wealth, and reputation—all the things that he values for themselves. (2) The spiritual man acknowledges the spiritual and the celestial as being the True and the Good, but the basis of his acts is still a principle of faith, not pure love. The ends that influence him concern the life beyond this world. His "combat for the soul" is a victorious combat; he knows only purely internal bonds, the bonds of conscience. (3) The celestial man has not only knowledge but also direct *perception* of the spiritual and the celestial. He acknowledges no other faith but that which proceeds from love, which is the principle of his action. The ends that influence him concern the Lord and His realm. He has nothing more to combat; he *is* the victorious one, he is the *free being*. He knows no other bonds but his perceptions of the Good, which is the order of heavenly love, and of the True, which proceeds from that love.[84]

From the entirety of these characteristics, a precise feature stands out: that direct, immediate *perception*, which is the divine grace imparted to the celestial man. This is the central theme of the drama of the anthropology, of the history of Adam. The spiritual man is still only the sixth day of creation; he is the eve of the seventh day, the eve of the Sabbath. When he becomes celestial man, he *is* the seventh day, the Sabbath, the "work of God," because the Lord alone fought for him during the six days, that is, created, formed, and made him.[85] Thenceforth the external man obeys the internal man and is in his service; the celestial man is the "perfect man," complete by means of the life of faith and the life of love; the life of faith prepares him, but it is the life of love that makes him man, for a man is such as is his love, even as to his intelligence and his faith.[86]

The celestial man *is* himself the garden in which it is said that the Lord set man. It is permitted him to know what is good and what is true by means of all possible *perceptions*. However, although the garden is *he*, it is not *his*; all his perceptions are activated in him by the Lord; the day when he considers that he can perceive from himself, that is, when he will want to investigate the *arcana* of faith and of the suprasensory worlds, relating them to sensory things, to "scientific" things, which are knowledges of the "external memory," on that day the death of his celestial nature will occur.[87] Then there will be an interruption, in his subtle spiritual being, of that mysterious internal respiration, the nature of which we have no idea about today, and that is why the substantial existence of something like the *spirit* seems improbable to so many people, since they confuse what is connoted by the word *spiritus* with the breath of their physiological respiration.[88]

These lines sketch out the meaning of the first drama of this humanity. Like the drama itself, they concern the entire *Antiquissima Ecclesia*, which was the seventh day. At the same time, all the interior realities (the *interiora*) of the Word are of such a nature that whatever is said in it of the *Ecclesia* may also be said of each individual member, for if every individual were not himself an *Ecclesia*, a temple of the Lord, he could not be a part of the *Ecclesia*, nor could he be what is signified by the "temple"; for that reason the entire *Antiquissima Ecclesia* is called *Homo* in the singular.[89] It is in this monadological reciprocity of the All and the "every" that will now be seen the internal sense of the drama that began with the decline of the seventh day, a drama that was by no means the "drama of the flesh," as a popular and common exegesis would have it, but a drama—*the* drama—of human understanding and consciousness. On this point there is a striking accord between Swedenborgian exegesis and Isma'ili exegesis.

However, as a prelude to the explanation of the internal sense of this drama, it is necessary above all to bear in mind the technical details that Swedenborg gives regarding what he designates as *perception*. There is no knowledge today of what it is, he says, because it concerns a certain internal sensation, a spiritual sensitivity[90] that evidently can be only a paradox for all agnostic rationalism. But the celestial men of the *Antiquissima Ecclesia* knew very well what it was, and we have already been told that they participated in the privilege of this angelic perception (whereas the spiritual man has conscience, but does not have perception, and the dead man does not even have conscience). Perceptions are of two kinds: one consists in perceiving directly truth or falsity, the being or non-being of a thing, and in perceiving also the source itself of the thought; there is another kind, common to angels and spirits, which consists in perceiving the quality of a being who comes toward them, simply by means of his approach and by a single one of his ideas.[91]

With Swedenborg, however, the theory of this perception proceeds from a profoundly and authentically mystical sentiment. It presupposes a transparency, a perfect translucence, in the sense that the being to whom it is imparted knows that in each of his acts of understanding and thinking, willing and acting, the active Subject is in fact the Lord Himself.[92] In a way, it is the substitution of *cogitor* for the Cartesian *cogito*, and it is this which makes of the celestial man a paradise, that is, the "garden of the Lord." On the other hand, there are spirits who cannot do otherwise than to assume that they are the real agents of their acts of understanding, of their intelligence, and of their wisdom; and that if all this were to "inflow" into them, they would be deprived of life, they would not exist, and it would be another who was thinking, not they themselves. For these, it is impossible to understand what *perception* is and what life is, that is, the mysterious influx from the spiritual world, which is the light of every natural man.[93] Not being able to understand it, they withdraw into an illusory self, and the more they cling to it, the more they become dark and opaque to that light. They can no longer recover what it is in them that is their true self; they commit an act of mortal confusion about the human *proprium*; they are expelled from the garden that man himself was, in his being, in the state of divine transparency. But since man *was* that garden, to be expelled from it is nothing less for man than to be expelled from himself. This was the decadence of the *Antiquissima Ecclesia*, that is, of the celestial person, whose posterity was finally suffocated by the Flood.

5. The Spiritual Sense of the History of Adam

At the risk of oversimplification, it is necessary here to summarize Swedenborg's long and very dense pages as concisely as possible. Inasmuch as the *place* of a spiritual being is his internal state, the garden or paradise is, therefore, the celestial man himself, his internal state. The trees of that garden are all his possible *perceptions* of love and intelligence, of the Good and the True; we have just seen the technical meaning of this, and it is decisive for what follows. But among these trees there is one that he must not touch, on pain of death. On the level of spiritual hermeneutics, what does this mean? The celestial man, the man of the *Antiquissima Ecclesia*, had a direct perception of all the things of heaven through direct relations with the Lord and the angels, through revelations, visions, and dreams. What his mode of being permitted was the infinity of these perceptions derived from the divine Principle active in him, but what his mode of being prohibited was making these perceptions derive from himself and from the world, that is, inquiring into the things of heaven by means of the things of the senses, things called "scientifics," for then the celestial aspect of faith is destroyed. "A desire to investigate the mysteries of faith by means of the things of sense and of scientifics, was not only the cause of the fall of the posterity of the *Antiquissima Ecclesia*, as treated of in the second chapter of Genesis, but it is also the cause of the fall of every church; for hence come not only falsities, but also evils of life."[94]

Because the signification that thus bursts forth in this chapter of Genesis is perpetually immediate, let us be certain that we are clear as to what Swedenborg is saying. To understand heavenly things, suprasensory things, through the medium of sensory things is the approach of *analogical* understanding, of the perception of symbols. Of course, that is not what is referred to here—namely, the "science of correspondences," which is, we have seen, the preeminent science, the "science of sciences," which our theosopher, who was also a great man of science, himself practiced throughout his biblical commentaries, showing, for example, how the anatomy of the human brain can reveal for us analogically the topography of heaven as *Homo maximus*. No, the "fault" here would be precisely to forget the approach of analogical reasoning, the ***anaphora***, in order to require in its stead a scientific demonstration, reducing the analogous to the identical. The forbidden tree, the forbidden knowledge, is what the person of this world lays claim to when he requires that evidence for the suprasensory things of faith should be given to him by means of logical and empirical demonstration, without which he refuses them any adherence. Now, this requirement and the knowledge that it postulates proceed from man's ***proprium***, that is, from a person who is isolated from the Principle that is his life and his light. Such knowledge is also impossible because it would violate the order of things. It claims to assimilate rationally the suprasensory to the sensory, to eliminate the former by diminishing things to their sensory appearance or reducing them to their mathematical equivalent, which is the exact opposite of analogical—that is, hermeneutical—knowledge. This kind of knowledge receives its light from the Threshold that it crosses, where life is; the other sort proceeds only from the man of this world, remains on this side of the world, and bears death within itself.[95] In our day, we know quite well how certain forecasts termed "scientific" claim to describe the future of humanity, all the while ignoring everything about the Threshold that it is necessary for them to cross.

Now, it is this drama that is recounted by the first three chapters of Genesis, in the "history" of the ***Antiquissima Ecclesia*** from its first period, that of its flowering, when man was a celestial man, to the periods of its decline and disappearance. In order to grasp well the intentions of Swedenborgian hermeneutics, it is important to group together several essential features: the ***Antiquissima Ecclesia*** is the one that is designated as *Homo*, man in the abstract, who, as we already know, was created male ***and*** female, the signification of which we also know. The fall, the decline, and the disappearance of its posterity will be caused by an increasing attachment to what Swedenborg designates as the human ***proprium***. What connection is there, then, between these two representations of *Homo* and his ***proprium***?

In Swedenborg's vocabulary this latter word designates what belongs personally to an individual, his *selfhood*, his *ipseity* (*Selbstheit*). But this personal ipseity can be conscious of itself as inseparable from its Principle; it is then transparent to It; the life and light that are within it are the life and light of its Principle (this is the state that is expressed in Islamic spirituality by the saying "He who knows himself knows his Lord"). Or else, on the contrary, it can regard itself as though it existed independently of its Principle; it encloses itself within its fictitious autonomy, and at the same time it envelops itself with darkness and succumbs to annihilation and death. This is the key to the states of a person's ***proprium***, of his ipseity, according to which he acts—in conformity with the schema of the anthropology that we already know—from the celestial person, the spiritual person, or the material person. For the last, his own self, his ***proprium***, is absolutely everything; he does not imagine that he can continue to *be* if he loses it. For the second, the spiritual person, the feeling and the conviction that his Principle (the Lord) is "itself" the power of thinking and acting within him constitute, in a way, theoretical knowledge. Only the first, the celestial person, has the actual perception of it. In addition, although he has no desire for it, a ***proprium***, a self is truly given to him. It is a self like that of an angel, who, in supreme serenity, tastes the joy of governing himself by a self, a ***proprium***, "where there are all things that are of the Lord Himself." This is the true ***proprium***, the celestial Self, whereas that of the material person is the infernal self, hell itself.[96]

Thenceforth, events followed in rigorous succession: the posterity of the ***Antiquissima Ecclesia*** was not disposed to "dwell alone," that is, to be guided by this internal ***proprium***, this celestial Self. Like another ***Ecclesia*** later, it desired "to be among the nations." And because it desired this, it is said, "it is not good that the man should be alone" (Gen. 2:18).[97] Then a deep sleep fell upon the man (Gen. 2:21). This sleep is the state into which man was led to the point that it seemed to him that he possessed his own ipseity, that he was himself by means of himself, a state that is, in fact, a deep sleep, because while he is in it a person knows only that he lives, thinks, speaks, and acts from himself. When he begins to recognize the illusion of this, he rouses himself and wakes up as though emerging from a deep sleep.[98]

His waking from this sleep is, according to the biblical account, precisely the moment when the Lord, having fashioned one of the man's "ribs" into a woman, gave her to him (Gen. 2:22). The man was no longer alone. Of course, this is not a matter of some sort of surgical operation performed on the physical person of the individual Adam, but it is a matter of one of the most profound *arcana* that there is to meditate upon. This "rib," this element of the bony system that surrounds the chest and the heart, symbolizes the *proprium* of man, for as the angels of heaven see it, the *proprium*, the inmost self of man, appears as something bony, inanimate, like a dead and illusory thing, although it appears to man himself as something real. In fact, if life from his Principle (the Lord) is withdrawn, he falls dead, like a stone that falls. On the other hand, while he has within him—and knows that he has within him—life from his Principle (his Lord), his *proprium* no longer appears like bone to the angels, but seems to them living flesh, that flesh of which it is written that it took the place of the rib.[99] The woman, Eve, is, therefore, the *proprium*, the self of man, vivified by the Lord. That is why it is said not that the woman was "created," but that the man's "rib," his inmost self, his *proprium*, was fashioned into a woman.[100]

Let us return, then, to the previous exegesis[101] of the verse that concerned not Adam the individual, but *Homo*: "Male and female created He them" (Gen. 1:27). This exegesis teaches us that the masculine or man (*vir*) signifies or symbolizes the intelligence and everything that relates to it, consequently all things of wisdom and faith, while the feminine or woman signifies or symbolizes the will, consequently all things relating to love, and consequently relating to life, since life proceeds only from love.[102] Now, the power designated as will is the *nucleus*, the inmost heart of the human being. It is also said that the *Tree of Life*, which is love and from which faith derives, was "in the midst of the garden," that is, in the will, the heart of the internal man.[103] The feminine in the human being, or man's internal feminine, is, therefore, man's self, his *proprium*, but a self that is transparent to the Principle that vivifies it, for as celestial man is constituted on the morning of the seventh day, he is *Homo*, masculine and feminine (*mas femineus*, said the alchemists), that is—although the word was not uttered by Swedenborg—his spiritual constitution was androgynous (more precisely, in Swedenborgian terms, the spiritual constitution of the androgyne persists in the celestial *couple*, and that is why it is said that the two members of that couple are a single angel, each being the "reciprocal" of the other).[104]

Yet, the posterity of this *Homo* inclined to a desire that was the reason for the divine remark, "It is not good that the man should be alone." The formation of Eve thus symbolizes a process of exteriorizing, of objectifying, the *Self* of man, his *proprium*. That is why, in the first case, the feminine symbolizes the *Self*, the *proprium* of the *internal man*; thenceforth it symbolizes the *self*, the *proprium* of the *external man*. Meditating attentively upon Swedenborg's dense pages, one cannot but recall the commentary of Jacob Boehme on these same verses of the book of Genesis: how Adam was separated from *Sophia*, the "betrothed of his youth," his feminine self, and how Eve, his external feminine, was given to him in compensation. Eve is, then, before Adam's triumphant greeting, "the betrothed and wife." Adam-Eve is the sophianic couple, because Eve is the *proprium* of Adam, his *proprium* vivified by the Divine Presence; the Adam-Eve couple has the perception of all the Good of love and the Truth of faith and consequently possesses all wisdom and all intelligence in ineffable joy. This is what Swedenborg also finds signified in a verse of Jeremiah (31:22), where it is said: "Jehovah hath created a new thing in the earth, a woman shall compass a man." "It is the heavenly marriage that is signified in this passage also," he says, "where by a 'woman' is meant the Self, the *proprium* vivified by the Lord, of which woman the expression 'to compass' is predicated, because this *proprium* (this Self) is such that it encompasses, as a rib made flesh encompasses the heart."[105]

It is, however, just there, in that exteriorization of the *Self*, of the very ipseity or *proprium*, that the seed of danger is found. For the exteriorization of the *proprium* bore within itself the threat of desires for power, possessive desires that will be the destruction of celestial love and marriage. There is a striking parallelism between the drama of knowledge, the decline of human celestial consciousness, on one hand, as Swedenborg finds it signified in the first chapters of Genesis, and, on the other hand, the contrast between celestial love and debauched, infernal love, a contrast that inspired one of his most beautiful books, a book that is one of the richest in doctrine and in vision, and one that perhaps conceals the very foundation of his thought.[106] In the first celestial person, the internal person was so well differentiated from the external person that he perceived what belonged to the one and to the other, and he perceived how the Lord governs the external person by means of the internal person. His posterity, however, experienced an increasing desire for the *proprium* that belongs to the external person; such a radical alteration ensued that people no longer even perceived the difference between the internal person and the external person, but imagined that one was indistinguishable from the other.[107] Herein is the origin of that yearning to possess a knowledge that gives possession even of the inaccessible object—inaccessible to all knowledge other than a perception of the faith deriving from love. This yearning will be the death of the celestial person.

Such was the destiny of the third posterity of the *Antiquissima Ecclesia*: doubt. It was the destiny of people who maintained that there should be no faith in revealed things, that the existence of suprasensory spiritual worlds should not be accepted, except on condition that they were seen and perceived by common empirical knowledge.[108] The serpent, all kinds of serpents, in ancient times always designated those who had more trust in things presented to their senses than in revealed and suprasensory things. Their guile has been increased even more in our time, when they command an entire arsenal of knowledge called "scientific," which was unknown to the ancients. Sometimes it is the person who believes only his senses; sometimes it is the scientist, sometimes the philosopher. Here Swedenborg returns to his favorite theme, for his entire work—that of thinker and that of visionary—is testimony to the existence of a spiritual world more substantial, richer in images and forms, than the sensory world, whereas the deniers agree in rejecting its existence. They speak of the *spirit* in terms that they themselves do not understand. Cartesianism is particularly referred to here, for at best the philosopher consents in affirming that the spirit is of the *thought*, but then he removes from the spirit any substantiality that would make intelligible its independence with respect to the physical organism.[109] All, therefore, have profaned and continue to profane the Tree of Knowledge by maintaining that knowledge of suprasensory things may be subjected to postulates, laws, and demonstrations of empirical knowledge; but being unable to succeed, they declare that suprasensory things are nonexistent. It is precisely this that the celestial person of the *Antiquissima Ecclesia* refrained from doing at the beginning, but it is to this that his posterity succumbed.[110]

The change is indicated in an eloquent symbolism. At the beginning it is said (Gen. 2:9) that it was the Tree of Life that was in the center of the garden (the garden that man himself was). Then, during the conversation between the serpent and Eve, it is the Tree of Knowledge, the Tree of which one must not eat, that is situated in the center of the garden (Gen. 2:17, 3:3). It is no longer the same person—or the same human state. The person for whom the Tree of Life is in the center of the garden is the person in whom love predominates, the person for whom all knowledge and all wisdom proceed from love; it is also by means of love that such a person knows what faith is. When that generation had disappeared, there was the person for whom it was no longer the Tree of Life, but the Tree of Knowledge, that was in the center of the garden; the order of forces is reversed. It is no longer by means of love that people have knowledge of the things of faith, but it is by means of knowledges of faith they can also have knowledge of what love is, although among most there is rarely anything but a purely theoretical knowledge.[111]

This change, now, prepares the transition from antediluvan humanity to postdiluvian humanity, from the ***Antiquissima Ecclesia*** to the ***Antiqua Ecclesia***, from the celestial person to the spiritual person. The character of the first was totally different from that of the second; but something of the celestial seed of the first passed into the second, at least among those who were saved from what is designated as the Flood. The majority of the others proceeded toward the catastrophe. The ***fourth posterity*** was the one that "saw that the Tree was good for food"; it comprised those who allowed themselves to be seduced by the love of self, considered their ***proprium***, their self possessed in its own right and without transparence, as the source of their knowledge, and refused to believe in things revealed unless they saw them confirmed by the things of the senses, by logical or scientific knowledge. The ***nakedness*** that frightened them was precisely this: the surrender to their own ipseity; they found themselves stripped of intelligence and wisdom, because having believed that they had found the source of these in themselves, they found nothing there but the illusion of themselves. Thus, they were ***naked*** with respect to the True and the Good. The divine voice that they heard in the profaned garden was the interior voice, the last vestige of the celestial perception that they had possessed.[112] Here again we observe a remarkable convergence with Isma'ili gnosis, which interprets Adam's transgression as a breach in the relationship between *ẓāhir* and *bāṭin*, the external and the internal, the exoteric and the esoteric (see infra, § 2). Here, the breach is consummated with the *fifth posterity*, expelled from Paradise. Thereafter the Cherubim prevented access to it. Before them is the flame of a turning sword, which is the love of self and its senseless desires, its persuasions that push man to want to reenter Paradise, but he is continually flung back toward material and terrestrial things. For the Tree of Knowledge having been profaned, henceforth it is access to the Tree of Life that is forbidden.[113]

The states of the *Antiquissima Ecclesia* were in the following succession: (1) *Homo* in the state of oneness (masculine-feminine); (2) externalization of ipseity, of the *proprium*, signified by the formation of Eve; (3) the appearance of doubt; (4) the fall; (5) the expulsion from Paradise. The sixth and seventh posterities (Gen. 3:24) fell below the level of man; these exiles from Paradise, whose corruption was even greater because they fell from a higher degree, were the people of the Flood. Chapters 4 and 5 of the book of Genesis treat of the degeneration of the *Antiquissima Ecclesia*.[114] The ten names (Seth, Enoch, Kenan, etc.) that are spread out in the course of chapter 5, up to Noah,[115] signify not personal individuals, but doctrines, schools, stages in the decline of the *Antiquissima Ecclesia*, until finally no more remain except the small number described under the name of Noah as the *Nova Ecclesia*, reemerging from the darkness.[116]

6. *The Spiritual Sense of the History of Noah*

"And God saw that the wickedness of man was great in the earth, and that every imagination of the thoughts of his heart was only evil continually" (Gen. 6:5). In the literal sense the earth is where man is, but in the internal sense it is where love is, since man is such as is his love. Now, love is related to the basic and constitutive force or reality in man that is called will; this is why the earth signifies here the will itself of man; for it is from his basic willing that man is man, and not so much from his knowledge and intelligence, for these only proceed from his basic reality, to such an extent that he wants neither to know nor to understand what does not proceed from it.[117]

On the other hand, "Noah" signifies a *Nova Ecclesia*, which, we know, will be called *Antiqua Ecclesia* to distinguish it from both the one that preceded it, before the Flood, and the one that succeeded it.[118] But the state of each differs profoundly from the other. We have already seen this difference described. The people of the *Antiquissima Ecclesia* had an immediate and direct perception of the Divine Good and of the Truth that proceeds from it. Those of the *Antiqua Ecclesia*, "Noah," no longer had direct perception, but they had a conscience and knowledge. Now, direct perception designates something other than conscience (vulnerable, if it is alone, to all sorts of doubts), and it also is the entire difference between the person that Swedenborg characterizes as the celestial person and the one that he designates as the spiritual person. For the first, it was by means of love that he was given to perceive all truths, those of the intelligence and of faith; in him, faith and knowledge were love. The person of the *Antiqua Ecclesia* became entirely different.[119]

As a prelude to his exegesis of chapter 6 of Genesis, Swedenborg repeats the warning that he has reiterated in his books. No one can see or understand the history of Noah in its true sense if he intends to apply himself exclusively to the sense of the letter, for here again the *style* that is historical in appearance is in reality symbolic, that is, metahistorical; it is not a matter of external events that would impose their course upon a historical narrative, it is a matter of events of the soul that are "historicized" in the form of external history.[120] The *Ecclesia* called Noah was the residue, the "remains," of the *Antiquissima Ecclesia* that was saved; it is that which is signified by the *Ark* and which is described in the measurements and the plan of the Ark.[121] How is the Ark used as a symbol to describe the formation of this new *Ecclesia*?

If it is its symbol, it is because everything that life still possessed and was worthy of possessing was received into it. But before it could be set up, it was necessary that the man of the new *Ecclesia* should pass through all sorts of ordeals, which are signified and described as the rising of the Ark upon the waters of the Flood, its floating and drifting on the surface, the long duration of the voyage, until this man finally became a spiritual man, a man who was liberated and free, to whom it could be said: "Go forth from the Ark."[122] The whole tale seems like the account of a long initiatory ordeal, and it is important to stress how closely Swedenborg's hermeneutics agree with what "traditional" sciences teach us, and how, for their part, the latter are confirmed by the testimony of visionary experiences that sustain his spiritual hermeneutics of the Bible.

The state of the person of the *Ecclesia* called Noah is thus that of a person in whom the organs of the internal person are closed, in the sense that they can no longer have direct communication with the spiritual world, with "Heaven," except in such a way that the person remains unconscious of it. Henceforth he must be instructed in it by external means, those of the senses and sensory things; he must learn how to transmute these into symbols. This will be possible, thanks to what has been preserved of immediate revelations or "celestial ideas" of the *Antiquissima Ecclesia*; these will be the *doctrinalia* preserved by Enoch, of whom it is said that "God took him" (Gen. 5:24), because these *doctrinalia*—at the moment when "he was taken"—were not of use or purpose to anyone.[123]

In addition, the state of humanity represented in the Noah *Ecclesia* as a residue, "remains" saved from the original celestial *Ecclesia* among the exiles from Paradise, is revealed in the profound sense of these words: "And the Lord shut him [Noah] in[to the Ark]" (Gen. 7:16). The man Noah could no longer have interior communication with heaven. In fact, a communication remained possible, for the degrees and modalities of communication with the spiritual world are limitless; even an evil or malevolent person has one, however weak and remote it may be, by means of the angels who are near him, otherwise the person would not even be able to exist. Since "the door was shut," though, the spiritual worlds have not been open as they were for the man of the *Antiquissima Ecclesia*. Afterward, many people, such as Moses, Aaron, and numerous others, had conversations with spirits and angels, but in an entirely different manner. The barrier is of such a kind and the reason for it is so deeply hidden that the person of our time does not even know that there are spirits, much less that there are angels with him, and he imagines that he is completely alone when there are no visible companions present and that he is thinking by himself, that is, only by means of the deliberation of his *proprium*, his illusory self. The reason for this occultation is profound, and Swedenborg analyzes it in an observation that is no less profound. It is that people have so inverted the orders of life, have succumbed to the obsession of wanting to judge suprasensory things only on the basis of sensory things and according to their laws, that in this state any manifestation of the things of heaven would be extremely perilous for them; it would lead inevitably to profanation and blasphemy, to the confusion of the sacred and the profane (the spiritual and the social), which, if it occurs in a spirit, places him in community with infernal spirits in the other world.[124]

A person acquires a life, *his* life, by means of all the things that he professes, his inner convictions. Those that do not affect him are as though nonexistent *for* him, since it is *by means of* him that they must exist. Thus, the unpardonable profanation of holy things is not possible except for someone who has once been convinced of them and has then come to deny and reject them. Those who do not acknowledge them and whom they do not affect may always come to know; it is as though they had not known, for their case is the same as that of people who accept things that have no existence. This is why the mysteries of faith are not revealed except when the state of men is such that they no longer believe in them and consequently cannot profane them. This is the "total devastation."[125] It was therefore necessary for the antediluvians to be expelled from Paradise, for they had known; it was necessary that men should no longer know. Thus, there is an extraordinary symmetry between the man Adam driven out to the exterior of Paradise and the man Noah entering into the *interior* of the Ark that is then closed upon him. In this there is also a profound way of expressing the necessity for esoterism. The man Noah does not "come forth from the Ark" until he has overcome the ordeal of the Flood.

In order, then, to understand in what the Flood consisted, as well as to understand the transition from the person of immediate spiritual perception (*Antiquissima Ecclesia*) to the person of conscience (*Antiqua Ecclesia*), and with this transition the necessity for esoterism, it is essential to bear in mind the leitmotiv that Swedenborg stresses particularly in this regard, namely, the physiology of the celestial person compared to that of the spiritual person. The first, we already know, had, aside from his external respiration, a totally silent internal respiration. Among themselves, people did not communicate so much by means of articulated words, as we do, but they did so by ideas, as the angels do. Swedenborg knew that what he formulated in this way would seem incredible, and yet it is so. He also knew that it would be difficult, and perhaps futile, to describe the mode of perception made possible by this internal respiration, for it would not be understood. When the external respiration alone remained, requiring language in words uttered and articulated, in which ideas are delimited and captive, the human state was entirely changed. This is the reason that people may no longer have immediate perception; people no longer had anything but conscience or, at best, something intermediate between immediate perception and conscience, an intermediary that is still known in our time. In brief, however, the result was that people could no longer be instructed directly by means of the internal person; it was necessary to pass through the external person.[126]

Expressed in these terms, the anthropological change allows us to have an idea of the drama. A double danger threatens man: the danger of suffocation by spiritual things, a knowledge of which required that mysterious internal respiration, for he can no longer "breathe" them; and suffocation caused precisely by the absence of the things that had been his life. This double suffocation is the *Flood*. Throughout the Sacred Books, water or waters are symbols of things that relate to intelligence and knowledge, and, as a corollary, to lack of knowledge, for falsification, lies, and deception pertain negatively to knowledge.[127] (Again, let us note in this spiritual exegesis a striking convergence with the Isma'ili gnosis of the Flood; see infra, § 3.)

The Flood, in its internal signification and its spiritual truth, is not a geological cataclysm, nor is it a cataclysm affecting the physical totality of the earth, of its telluric mass. We know what the designation *earth* symbolizes: those who constituted the last posterity of the *Antiquissima Ecclesia*. In them there was still a "breath of life," albeit in a germinal state, that they retained from their distant ancestors, although they themselves were no longer in the life of faith proceeding from love. Possessed by insane desires, abominable appetites, they immersed the things of faith in them; the deceitful persuasions of their being extinguished and suffocated all truth and all good, rendering inoperative the residue, the "remains" of life that they still had. But in suffocating that, in drowning and stifling the internal person and his respiration, they destroyed themselves and expired. Such was the death of the antediluvians, for no one succeeds in living, *living* in the sense that excludes death, without a minimum of conjunction with Heaven.[128]

This conjunction is what maintained the man Noah in the Ark, by preserving the "breath of life" there. But it was at the cost of a long ordeal, a long combat and severe tribulations, before he could achieve the regeneration refused by those who preferred the desolation of their own devastation. All the numbers that are given—the forty days of the Flood, the one hundred fifty days of the submersion of the earth, the age of Noah, as well as the date of the event ("the six hundredth year of Noah's life")—have a symbolic, and consequently initiatory, signification. Thus, the signification is current, present. For the angels of Heaven it is all the same whether a thing is past, present, or to come: "What is to come is present, or what is to be done is done."[129]

We understand, then, the human ordeal symbolized in that of the man Noah or the *Ecclesia* Noah. What our theosopher was witness to in the course of his "visions in the Spirit" was the influx of infernal spirits as something impulsive, furious. Their object was the total subjugation of man, not only to make man one of them, but to reduce him to nothing. People are not free of their domination and their yoke except at the cost of the combat that the Lord gives through the agency of the angels that are with everyone. As long as this internal combat lasts, man remains, for his salvation, in the Ark, ringed by the waters of the Flood, shaken by ordeals, that is, by the attempts of the evil spirits. At the end of his regeneration, "God spake unto Noah, saying, Go forth from the Ark" (Gen. 8:15-16). This address by God to Noah is nothing other than the divine Presence henceforth recovered, for so far as He is present, God speaks with man; and His Presence implies freedom. The more the Lord is present, the more people are free, that is, the more a person is in the state of love, the more freely he acts.[130] Noah, then, may leave the Ark; he has overcome the ordeal of the Flood. We have been told that the celestial person is called the "Victorious."

Of necessity, we have been limited here to these few themes illustrating the spiritual history of humanity, a recurrent history, always present, since in the spiritual world the moments of time are nothing other than successive internal states; a reversible time, for it is not a homogeneous quantitative time, a time to which some unit of external measurement would relate, subject to the irreversible progression of numbers. What we have been able to gather here, in relation to Swedenborg's immense work, is not even a drop of water in relation to the ocean. Nevertheless, it has allowed us to penetrate sufficiently into what constitutes the reality and the essence of a *spiritual event*, in order to understand how the truth of this event controls all the approaches of spiritual hermeneutics, that is, the comprehension of a sense that, as such, can absolutely not be *closed* and consequently cannot be *enclosed* in the literal sense of a *history* henceforth "past and gone."

In this way we have approached somewhat more closely to what constitutes the phenomenon of the Sacred Book, the Revealed Book, and to what distinguishes it from every profane book, namely, the exegesis that it imposes: to understand its *true* sense, a sense that, as it is *true*, is the *present* sense. It is here that there is profound accord between the spiritual hermeneutists of the Bible and the spiritual hermeneutists of the Qur'ān—the more easily because the Qur'ān gathers much data from the Bible, particularly about the history of Adam and the history of Noah, themes to which our examination of spiritual hermeneutics has limited itself, for the time being. This profound accord in the quest for the true sense of the Sacred Book arranges for us the modulation that will allow us to pass from one subject to another. We do not have to search very far for that transition. It is best indicated to us in the response given to one of his acquaintances by the Fifth Imām of the Shi'ites, Imām Moḥammad al-Bāqir (A.H. 57/A.D. 676-A.H. 115/A.D. 733), who declared: "If the revelation of the Qur'ān only had meaning with regard to the person or group of people as a result of whom one or another verse was revealed, then the entire Qur'ān would be dead today. No! The Sacred Book, the Qur'ān, is alive, it will never die; its verses will be fulfilled among the people of the future, as they have been fulfilled among those of the past."[131]

This remark by the Imām admirably anticipates and defeats, before the fact, the trap of what we call today *historicism*, that is, the systematic attitude which, by making the significance of the Sacred Book *captive* to the date of its material composition, stifles any potential for a significance that goes beyond that "past." We will see that, on both sides, the mirage of these opinionated so-called historical solutions is escaped by means of the *presence* of spiritual universes that symbolize with each other, by means of a comparable architecture, and in relation to which what we call history is a *ḥikāyat*, a "history" that is a *mimēsis*. Such will be, in fact, the Shi'ite and Isma'ili vision of things.

II. Isma'ili Gnosis

1. Shi'ite and Isma'ili Hermeneutics

It is only possible here to mention allusively, in a few words, what constitutes the essence of Shi'ism in general, both Twelve-Imām Shi'ism and Seven-Imām Shi'ism or Isma'ilism; for more details, the reader is referred to our previously published works.[132] The Shi'ite religious phenomenon concerns us here in the first place because it differs from Sunni Islam insofar as it postulates, even as its foundation, spiritual hermeneutics of the Sacred Book, the Qur'ān. This exigency derives from a theological and theosophical conception that constitutes the originality and the richness of Shi'ism, so that the question that was posed early in Sunni Islam regarding the created or uncreated nature of the Qur'ān appeared ill posed in this context, because it was deprived of the metaphysical horizon that it presupposes. It is to Shi'ism that Islamic thought is indebted for a prophetology and a prophetic philosophy. This prophetology is characterized by the fact that the mission of the prophet-messengers (simultaneously *Nabī* and *Rasūl*), instructed to reveal a Sacred Book to men, is inseparable from the *walāyat*, that is, the spiritual qualification of the Imāms, successors to the Prophet, as "Friends of

God" (*Awliyā' Allāh*), to whom is entrusted, since they are "Spiritual Guides" and "Sustainers of the Book," the task of initiating men into its *true* sense.

Prophecy and Imāmate (or *walāyat*) correspond to a double cosmic movement: *mabda'* and *ma'ād*, genesis and return, descent and ascent to the origin. To this double movement correspond, on one hand, *tanzīl*, Revelation—the act of *sending down* the Sacred Book, the letter of which the prophet is instructed to express (the *sharī'at*, the Law, the positive religion)—and, on the other hand, *ta'wīl*, which is the act of *bringing back* the letter of Revelation to its true sense—spiritual *exegesis*, which is the function of the Imām. This true sense is the spiritual sense, the *ḥaqīqat* or Idea. As one of the greatest Isma'ili theosophers of Iran, Nāṣir-e Khosraw (eleventh century), wrote: "Positive religion [*sharī'at*] is the exoteric aspect of the spiritual Idea [*ḥaqīqat*], and the spiritual Idea is the esoteric aspect of positive religion; positive religion is the symbol [*mathal*], the spiritual Idea is that which is symbolized [*mamthūl*]."[133]

All of Shi'ism, considered as Islamic esoterism, is in agreement on these essential concepts. There are, however, a certain number of internal differences between the two principal forms of Shi'ism: Twelve-Imām Shi'ism, on one hand, which is still called *Imāmism* and which, for the past five centuries, has been the official religion of Iran; and, on the other hand, Seven-Imām Shi'ism or Isma'ilism, which itself now includes two main branches. The difference relates essentially to the concept of the Imāmate, and consequently to the structure of the esoteric hierarchies, and thus to the application of spiritual hermeneutics. Twelve-Imām Shi'ism limits the number of Imāms ("Spiritual Guides") to twelve persons in all, who, together with the Prophet himself and his daughter Fāṭima, the origin of their lineage, form the pleroma of the "Fourteen Pure Ones" (in Persian, *Chahārdeh-Ma'ṣūm*). Together, they are the earthly manifestation of the *Ḥaqīqat moḥammadīya*, eternal prophetic

Reality, in its double aspect (*Logos-Sophia*) of the exoteric manifested in law-giving prophecy and the esoteric manifested in the Imāmate. With the Twelfth Imām, the Imāmate withdraws into occultation (*ghaybat*). The Imām is never absent from this world, of which he is the mystic pole (*qoṭb*), without which mankind would not be able to continue to exist, but he was "removed" from this world, as were, according to our Western traditions, the holy Grail and its guardian. Consequently, in both cases, the esoteric hierarchy itself lives in strict incognito; we are not able to say *who* its members are, and they are not permitted to reveal themselves.[134]

The spiritual hermeneutics of Imāmite theosophy is applied in terms of the Manifestation of eternal prophetic Reality, that is, of the Fourteen Pure Ones, to the different degrees of the hierarchy of the spiritual universes preceding our world of sensory phenomena.[135] This Manifestation is accompanied by a state of the Divine Word, the Book or eternal Qur'ān, varying according to each of these universes. To simplify matters, we will say that four of these are distinguished, symbolized by the "four Lights of the Throne" that are mentioned in traditions extending back to the holy Imāms themselves: there are, below the pleroma of the *Ḥaqīqat moḥammadīya*, the world of pure Lights (*'ālam al-Anwār*), the world of the *jabarūt* [the world of the Cherubim, of the Divine Names of God], symbolized by white light; the world of Spirits (*'ālam al-Arwāḥ*), the world of the higher *Malakūt* [the world of the *Animae coelestes*, the esoteric aspect of the visible heavens], symbolized by yellow light; the world of Souls (*'ālam al-Nofūs*), symbolized by green light, and including the *mundus imaginalis*, the world of subtle bodies and the emerald cities; and the world of material bodies (*'ālam al-ajsām*), symbolized by red light (it can be seen that the first three are, respectively, in correspondence with the three degrees of Heaven, as Swedenborg describes it: celestial angels, spiritual angels, and angelic spirits).

Each of these worlds is the internal, the esoteric (*bāṭin*) in relation to the one or ones below it, but it is itself the exoteric (*ẓāhir*), the containant, the rind (*qishr*), in relation to those that are above it. Thus, in a way, an esoterism to the fourth power is reached. Each of these four degrees is capable, besides, of a sevenfold resonance. Another schema relates the exoteric or *ẓāhir* to the entirety of the visible world (from celestial Spheres to minerals); the esoteric or *bāṭin* to the Fourteen Pure Ones in their earthly Manifestation; the esoteric of the esoteric (*bāṭin al-bāṭin*) to their epiphany in the higher spiritual universes; *ta'wīl*, as the first exegesis, leads back, on one hand, to the *microcosm* that is the human individual, and, on the other hand, to the *mesocosm*, to the middle world, which is that of alchemical operation. These few premises suffice to make understandable why our thinkers declare that meditation on the Qur'ān is inexhaustible. An entire library would be necessary in order to realize integrally the totality of the hermeneutic plan for the totality of verses in the Qur'ān.[136] Moreover, it is the function of the Hidden Imām, at the time of his appearance, to reveal the esoteric sense of all the Divine Revelations; it is precisely this which is the *Qiyāmat* (resurrection).

However close the affinities may be, things appear somewhat differently in Isma'ilism. Up to the time of the Sixth Imām, Ja'far al-Ṣādiq (d. 148/765), one of the great figures in Shi'ite Islam, there was only one Shi'ism. For very complex reasons, one group of his followers (his "Shi'ites") then became attached to the Imāmic line represented in the person of his oldest son, Imām Isma'il, whose premature death caused so many difficulties; for that reason, they were called Isma'ilis.[137] The remaining followers transferred their allegiance to his other son, Mūsā Kāẓem, as Seventh Imām; these were the Imāmites or Twelve-Imām Shi'ites. In fact, under the appearance of historical contingencies, the secret law that gives rhythm to spiritual history imposed itself in both instances: in one case, the number twelve (each of the six great prophets had his twelve Imāms); in the other, among the Isma'ilis, the number seven (the succession of each prophet passes through seven Imāms or several heptads of Imāms).

Isma'ilism, the preeminent Islamic gnosis, experienced the most formidable and paradoxical ordeal that an esoteric religion may undergo, when it gained a temporal and political triumph with the Fātimid dynasty of Egypt. Its eschatological essence would otherwise have required that this triumph be the end of the story. Instead of stopping there, however, external history led to the schism resulting from the death of the Eighth Fātimid caliph, al-Mostanṣir bi'llah (487/1094). Today, Isma'ilism is still divided into two major branches: one perpetuates the Fātimid tradition, and for it, too, the Imām has entered into occultation with the last Fatimid of Cairo; the other branch, the adherents of the Aga Khan, emerged from the Iranian reform of Alamūt.

Alamūt! The stronghold lost in the high solitary summits of the Elburz mountain chain, to the southwest of the Caspian Sea, where, on 8 August 1164, the Great Resurrection (*Qiyāmat al-Qiyāmāt*) was proclaimed. We should celebrate its eight hundredth anniversary this month [August 1964] (at least according to the solar calendar).[138] Undoubtedly, though, a proclamation of this type pertains to that spiritual history, the events of which occur unnoticed by external official history, because their implication cannot be suspected by historians whose attention is given exclusively to the latter. In any case, the proclamation of the Great Resurrection was intended to be the triumph of absolute spiritual hermeneutics, since it purely and simply abolished the *sharī'at* and its observances, in order to permit the reign of the spiritual Idea (the *ḥaqīqat*) alone to subsist. Here again, the impatience of the soul provoked a premature anticipation of eschatology, although the Event proclaimed on 8 August 1164, which passed unobserved by the external history of our world, perhaps had the sense of one of those *judgments* "in Heaven," about which we have heard Swedenborg speak. On the other hand, the Shi'ism of the Fātimid tradition, as well as Twelve-Imām Shi'ism, continued carefully to maintain (as did

Swedenborg) the coexistence of the exoteric and the esoteric, for as long as the human condition remains what it is in the present world, the soul cannot manifest itself without being contained in a material body.

For Isma'ilism as well, the literal sense, the external appearance, the exoteric containant (*ẓāhir*) conceals a plurality of internal senses ordered in a hierarchy of universes that symbolize with each other. The Principle (*Mobdi'*), Divine Silence and Abyss, remains, as in every gnosis—and as with Swedenborg—strictly inaccessible, Super-Being (*hyperousion*) beyond being and nonbeing. From the First Archangelic Intelligence that emerges from this Silence, raised up in being as *Deus revelatus*, proceeds the entire supreme pleroma of the primordial Establishment (*'ālam al-Ibdā'*), formed of hierarchical archangelic Intelligences. A cosmogony that is simultaneously speculative and dramatic posits that from one of these Intelligences, our demiurge, is the origin of our physical universe, the *macrocosm*, including the astronomical sky and the world of Elements; the *microcosm*, or world of man, the structure of which is homologous to that of the macrocosm; and finally, an intermediary world, the *mesocosm*, which is the spiritual world constituted by the esoteric community on earth.

The idea of the macrocosm, which is that of the cosmic Man, is well known in other gnostic and theosophical systems; it is the theme of the Human Form as archetype of the universes (Greek μακρανθρῶπος, Arabic *Insān kabīr*). We have mentioned above that it is a dominant theme in the Swedenborgian topography of the spiritual universes (*Homo maximus*), and the theme seems to us to be in particular accord with the Isma'ili idea of the Imām to come, the last Imām of our *Aiōn*, as Imām of the Resurrection (*Qā'im al-Qiyāmat*), for everything upon which speculative gnosis has meditated in the theme of the *Anthrōpos* is found collected together in the person of the Imām as *Anthrōpos* in the absolute sense. Herein is, in fact, his divinity (his *lāhūt*), that is, the human form arising in its truth and its integrality; in its archangelic splendor it is the "Temple of Light" (*Haykal nūrānī*), constituted by all the "forms of light" of the initiates of the esoteric community, the future temple of their apotheoses, where each of them assumes a rank and a role respectively analogous to those of each of the organs and members in the physical human body.[139]

The hierarchical structure of the *mesocosm*, or of the esoteric community in our world, symbolizes with that of the "Temple of Light," as it symbolizes with the hierarchical structure of the astronomical sky, and as the latter also symbolizes with the hierarchy of the invisible heavens of the archangelic Pleroma. Isma'ili metaphysics is characterized by this fundamental hierarchy of being, and the springboard of its spiritual hermeneutics is essentially the strict correspondence between the degrees of the celestial hierarchy and the degrees of the earthly esoteric hierarchy. The mesocosm also concerns anthropology and angelology simultaneously, since to enter into the mystic community on earth, as a member of the *corpus mysticum*, is to enter into the "virtual paradise," and thereby to allow the potential angelhood in the human being to achieve actual angelhood after death. Here, too, there is another concept that is in profound accord with Swedenborgian anthropology.

Certainly, the developments and vicissitudes of Isma'ili thought have led to modifications in the conception of the detail of these hierarchies. In its most complete form, as it is presented, for example, in the work of Ḥamīd Kermānī (d. about 408/1017), the schema agrees with that of the Avicennian philosophers. To the Ten Archangelic Intelligences of the supreme Pleroma (each of these Intelligences itself containing an entire pleroma), corresponds the visible astronomical sky and the grades of the esoteric hierarchy.[140] Before and afterward, less complex schemas were known, especially in the work of the Isma'ili author whom we will be questioning here regarding the Isma'ili conception of the spiritual sense of the history of Adam and the history of Noah.

Qāżī No'mān, who lived in the tenth century, was a prolific writer; among other works, we are indebted to him for one entitled *Asās al-Ita'wīl* ("the book of the foundation of esoteric exegesis, or of spiritual hermeneutics"),[141] devoted especially to our subject here. The book is presented, in the form of esoteric hermeneutics of the Qur'ān, as an account of the spiritual history of the prophets, more specifically the six great lawgiving prophets whose names designate the six great periods in the cycle of prophecy: Adam, Noah, Abraham, Moses, Jesus, and Muḥammad. The author assembles all the qur'ānic data that concern each of these prophets, and indicates the esoteric sense hidden in the events, words, or acts related about that prophet.

Everything is transposed strictly onto the spiritual plane. Let us be more explicit. Where Swedenborg speaks of an *Ecclesia* embracing all the visible and invisible universes, all the times of our history and of metahistory, the Isma'ili thinkers speak of the *da'wat.* Literally, the word means "convocation," "call." This refers to a Call, a Convocation that begins "in Heaven" with the Call addressed by the First Intelligence to the entire original pleroma. Prophecy thus begins "in Heaven" and, following the "drama in Heaven" that is the source of the cosmogony, it is perpetuated on earth from cycle to cycle. The *da'wat*, the Isma'ili Convocation, is nothing other than the particular form taken by the Convocation or eternal *da'wat* in this final period of our cycle or *Aiōn*, the period of Muḥammadan prophecy and of the Imāmate that succeeds it. In that sense, the *da'wat* is, in short, the Isma'ili *Ecclesia*.

Let us, then, remember essentially this: what is the object of this Convocation, this Call or *da'wat*? It is the call to *tawḥīd*, the call to recognize the Unicity and Unity of the Divine Unique. In fact, in this again is the exoteric sense, since the Principle is beyond our affirmations and our negations, which can only attain to a *Deus revelatus seu determinatus.* What, then, does the initiate deny by the negation *lā ilāha* (*Nullus Deus* [there is no god]), and what does he affirm by affirming *illā Al-lāh* (*nisi Deus* [but God])?[142] What is proclaimed and revealed by the esoteric sense of these words that compose the *shahādat* (the attestation of the Unique) is precisely the ranks of the double celestial and earthly hierarchy that proceeds from the primordial Theophany, from the First Archangelic Intelligence as *Deus revelatus.* In other words, to escape from the double snare of agnosticism (*ta'ṭīl*) and anthropomorphism (*tashbīh*) is to recognize the mystery of the Unique in each of the Uniques, celestial and earthly, such that the Unique is determined for each by the rank that precedes it. These Uniques are thus the members, the dignitaries (*ḥodūd*) of the *da'wat*, in heaven and on earth. They are the *dramatis personae* of events and vicissitudes of the *da'wat*, that is, of the secret spiritual history of humanity that is the esoteric sense (the *bāṭin*, the *ḥaqīqat*) of the apparent letter of the Qur'ān, the *dramatis personae* of which, however, remain unknown to whoever is attached only to the material data of the visible history.

Our present subject does not require us to enter into detail regarding these hierarchies. Let us recall briefly how the analysis of the *shahādat* (the testimony, the profession of faith) permits the Isma'ili authors to deduce the principal figures from it. The *four* words that compose it refer to the two supreme celestial "dignitaries," the First Intelligence and the First Soul (*Sābiq* and *Tālī*), and to the two supreme earthly "dignitaries" who correspond to them: the Prophet and the Imām. That is why it is said that the *shahādat* is the "key to paradise," and our authors indicate that the four words that compose it and the four branches of the Christian cross are together the symbols of the same realities.[143] The *seven* syllables that express the *shahādat* refer to the seven Imāms who succeed each other in the course of a period of prophecy. The *twelve* letters that compose the Arabic writing of the *shahādat* are the symbols of the twelve dignitaries called *Ḥojjat* (proof, pledge) or *lawāḥiq* (devotees, assistants) who permanently form, from one generation to another, the close entourage of the Imām.[144] They are doubled by twelve others called Wings (*ajniḥa*); these are the *dāʿīs*, the secret emissaries assigned to propagate the Call, the *daʿwat*, in each of the twelve *jazīra* (regions) into which, ideally at least, the world is divided. Such is the order of things presented by Qāżī Noʿmān, the author whom we are following here, and it is sufficient to understand the spiritual dramaturgy concealed under the external history of Adam and Noah, the double theme to which we must limit ourselves here, before saying a few words about Ismaʿili Christology.

2. *The Esoteric Sense of the History of Adam*

We have just described the twelve esoteric "dignitaries" designated as *Ḥojjat* of the Imām. Their establishment extends back to the initiation of the one who was the *first Adam* on earth, the universal primordial Adam (*Adam al-awwal al-kollī*), *pananthrōpos* who must not be confused with the *partial* Adam, initiator of our present cycle of prophecy. He must also not be confused with the spiritual Adam (*Adam rūḥānī*), celestial *Anthrōpos* or Angel of humanity, who was the protagonist of the drama that occurred in the Pleroma, the drama of which our earthly history, understood as hierohistory or spiritual history, is after all the *ḥikāyat* (the repetition, the imitation). Precisely the duration of earthly time, that of the cycles of hierohistory begins in the "delay of eternity" that occurred in the being of the celestial *Anthrōpos*, immobilized in doubt, in the vertigo of his own person. Earthly time must fill in the *delay*, which is "expressed in numbers" in the degradation in rank of the celestial Adam (from *third* to *tenth*). From cycle to cycle, from prophet to prophet, spiritual humanity, that which responds to the *daʿwat*, to the divine Call, tends to this "reconquest," the result of which is assured by the triumph that its Angel has already gained—and gained over himself. It is impossible here to say more about it or to explain how this "drama in Heaven" is the origin of the vertiginous succession of cycles on earth, where a "cycle of epiphany" (*dawr al-kashf*) and a "cycle of occultation" (*dawr al-satr*) alternate with each other. Evidently, the only one that may even be spoken about in full knowledge of cause is our present "cycle of occultation."[145]

What becomes apparent—and this is what interests us here—is the manner in which spiritual or esoteric hermeneutics of the Bible and the Qur'ān, particularly the hermeneutics of data common to both, tends in each case to discover the same secret that explains the present condition of man. In both instances, there is revealed essentially a drama of knowledge, a dislocation of the conscience, a fall of perceptive and cognitive powers, which cuts off the human being from his presence in other higher universes, in order to imprison him in the fate of his solitary presence in this world. If certain hermeneutic differences cannot but emerge, they are no less instructive, and a great many of them are not irreducible.

In both cases we find spiritual hermeneutics of the idea of the *hexaēmeron*, the six days of Creation, a profound symbol that an obsolete literalism can degrade to the point of making it puerile. We have seen that, in Swedenborg's works, the six degrees or stages of creation of the spiritual man are represented; the "seventh day" is the celestial man who symbolizes the *Antiquissima Ecclesia*. For Isma'ili gnosis, the *hexaēmeron* constitutes the six days of the creation of the *hierocosmos*, that is, of the religious and sacral universe (*'ālam al-Dīn*) of spiritual humanity. These "six days" are the six periods of our present cycle, each marked by the name of its prophet: Adam, Noah, Abraham, Moses, Jesus, Muḥammad. We are only at the sixth day of Creation; the "seventh day" (the Sabbath) will be the advent of the Imām of the Resurrection (*Qā'im al-Qiyāmat*).[146] But in both cases, celestial man, that is, the state of angelhood in act in man, is at the same time behind us and before us. *Behind us*: as the man of the "cycle of epiphany" before ours, in Isma'ili terms; this is like Swedenborg's morning of the seventh day. *Before us*: under the name of *Nova Hierosolyma*, in Swedenborgian terms; under the name of the Imām of the Resurrection, the seventh day of the *hexaēmeron* of the prophecy of which Adam was the first day, according to Isma'ili gnosis.

For Swedenborg, the seventh day is the establishment of man as celestial man, as earthly paradise, Garden of Eden, as the man in whom the perception of sensory things is concomitant with the immediate perception of suprasensory celestial things; it is this spiritual organism that will be dislocated, devastated, by the satanic suggestion to submit suprasensory things to the same laws as sensory things. In Isma'ili gnosis, the "earthly paradise" marks the descent of man on earth from the angelic state of the humanity of the previous "cycle of epiphany." The norm of his Knowing is the concomitance of the external and the internal, the exoteric (*ẓāhir*) and the esoteric (*bāṭin*), the perception of symbols. This concomitance will be broken, dislocated, by the suggestion of Iblīs-Satan, whose intervention is explained here by a preceding state of things. The consequence of the break is a denial of symbols, not so much on account of the exclusive preeminence accorded to sensory things thenceforth limited to themselves, as because of a pretension to direct attainment of the suprasensory. These are simply two complementary aspects of the same transgression, for in Isma'ili terms as well, the sensory, the exoteric, is condemned in both cases to signifying nothing but itself. Heaven is closed from that point on. In both cases, the departure, the exile from Paradise, the condition of our humanity, is foreshadowed as resulting from the desire to be present in this world—and exclusively in this world.

What, then, of the "prologue in Heaven" announcing, according to Isma'ili gnosis, the transition to our present "cycle of occultation"?[147] A verse of the Qur'ān states: "Behold, thy Lord said to the angels: 'I will create a vicegerent on earth.' They said: 'Wilt Thou place therein one who will make mischief therein and shed blood?...' He said: 'I know what ye know not'" (Qur'ān 2:28).[148] Other verses are explicit: "Behold, thy Lord said to the angels: 'I am about to create man from clay. When I have fashioned him (in due proportion) and breathed into him of My spirit, fall ye down in obeisance unto him.' So the angels prostrated themselves, all of them together. Not so Iblīs" (Qur'ān 38:71-74).

Isma'ili hermeneutics perceives in this verse a discourse addressed to his own by the last Imām of the "cycle of epiphany" that preceded our "cycle of occultation," Imām Honayd, the father of "our" Adam, whose decision is motivated by grave symptoms, the remembrance of which our memory has lost, and which marked the decline of the cycle. The Imām foresaw the cessation of this blessed state for his own, and the necessity to provide for the conditions of a new cycle, characterized by what we would call the "discipline of the *arcanum.*" This is what the angels "knew not."[149] But the angels whom he addresses do not constitute the totality of the angelic hierarchy. They are the twelve *lawāḥiq* (devotees, assistants), to whom we alluded earlier, and above whom there are superior angelic ranks. He chooses these twelve to be the companions of Adam, who is placed at their head. He informs them of his intention to establish Adam "on earth," and "to create him from clay." These two particulars indicate the transition from the celestial condition of the preceding cycle to the condition of the present cycle. In esoteric terms, clay signifies knowledge that is external or exoteric, opaque, material. Now, the angels were created in a state of subtle knowledge, of esoteric, internal, spiritual science, a knowledge that did not depend upon initiatory instruction (*ta'līm*), and that was exempt from ritual obligations and observances of the Law. In brief, "the human being created on earth" signifies the condition of a being who cannot thenceforth attain to the esoteric, to hidden spiritual reality, except through the intermediary of the exoteric, that is, by means of the knowledge of symbols.

This is emphasized by a *ḥadīth* (a tradition) illustrating the qur'ānic verse, which declares that Adam remained there, flung like an inert body, until God breathed His spirit into him, that is, until He had had breathed into him spiritual science, the science of the esoteric of things, that "science of Names" (Qur'ān 2:29), by means of which beings are promoted to their true being. It was because of this science that the angels gave their allegiance to Adam. In the interval, however, Iblīs had observed him and, being conscious of his own preeminence, cried: "He is nothing but emptiness." Thus he refused to bow down before Adam. Iblīs himself had been one of the angels of the preceding "cycle of epiphany" (one of the twelve *lawāḥiq*). When he is asked: "What prevents thee from prostrating thyself to one whom I have created with My hands? Art thou haughty? Or art thou one of the high ones?" (that is, according to the Isma'ili exegesis, "Are you one of the superior angels who are not concerned with the order given?"), "Iblīs said: I am better than he: Thou createdst me from fire, and him Thou createdst from clay" (Qur'ān 38:75-77, 7:11), which, in the esoteric sense, means: "You created me in the knowledge of the spiritual world, a knowledge that flashes by immediate divine influx (*al-'ilm al-ta'yīdī al-bāriq*), with which a material external object cannot coexist. Him, however, You created in a state of discursive, physical, material, opaque knowledge. How, then, should I bow down to him?" The secret of his refusal being thus divulged, Iblīs is cursed, expelled, cut off.[150]

There is here a profound intuition on the part of Isma'ili hermeneutics, when it connects the refusal of Iblīs and the creation of Eve, not at all because the Feminine plays the role of something satanic, as in a certain Christian asceticism, but quite the opposite. Iblīs, by refusing to admit that the esoteric may be organically linked to the exoteric, betrayed Adam; he deprived Adam of that esoteric and forbade him the perception of symbols. The profound idea is that the Feminine, Eve, was given to Adam in compensation for the betrayal by Iblīs, who became a fallen angel—because the Feminine *is* the esoteric. A qur'ānic verse (4:1) reminds men: "Your Lord created you from a single soul, and from this single soul He created his mate (his spouse, the female companion of this single soul)." The Isma'ili exegesis in no way sees here a physical anthropogenesis taking place in the physical order; what is spoken of is the spiritual history of man, the hidden sense of his drama. Man's companion and spouse, created from his single, solitary soul, signifies the creation of the *res religiosa* (*dīn*), and when an Isma'ili author utters or writes the word *dīn*, he thinks about "religion in truth," that is, esoteric religion. It is this esoteric, therefore, that is symbolized by Eve.[151]

This is why Qāżī No'mān is extremely sarcastic with regard to those literalists who imagine that God took advantage of Adam's sleep to practice some sort of surgical operation on his body.[152] They have read, he says, that God replaced one of Adam's "ribs" and made Eve, Adam's wife, from that rib, but they have understood nothing. The spiritual sense, though, is clear! Man has twelve ribs; they signify the twelve *lawāḥiq* or "angels" who had been chosen to surround Adam and help him,[153] in order to be twelve leaders, twelve spiritual princes (*noqabā'*). Iblīs was one of these twelve, but by his betrayal he cut himself off from their number. In that sense, Eve is given to Adam in compensation for Iblīs, and that is why Adam transmits to Eve, invests in her, all his knowledge of the esoteric. Thenceforth, Eve assumes and bears the esoteric, and that is why she is his wife; in terms of the Isma'ili hierarchy, she is his *Ḥojjat*, the *Ḥojjat* of the Imām Adam.

Something emerges here that is highly significant for the spiritual world of Isma'ilism: namely, that the esoteric is essentially the Feminine, and that the Feminine is the esoteric (the Self that is deep and hidden from man; the sense of the formation of Eve in Swedenborg's work should be compared here). That is why, in the bi-unity, the couple or dyad, that forms the prophet and the Imām, the prophet who is instructed to state the exoteric, the Law, symbolizes the masculine; the Imām, invested with the esoteric and the spiritual sense, symbolizes the feminine. It may be said of the Imām (or of his *Ḥojjat*, when the Imām has succeeded the Prophet) that he is the "spiritual mother" of the believers.[154] The consequences of this will be fundamental, when it involves interpreting the personages of spiritual history who are designated by feminine names, particularly for the entire chapter on Christology in Qāżī No'mān's book (see infra, § 4). The "Eternally feminine" refers here not to a quality of the secular state, but to a spiritual state, to a metaphysical status.

It is this masculine-feminine couple, Adam-Eve, that God established in the garden, the earthly paradise, "the most sublime thing that God has created."[155] To understand what this garden is and what the transgression was that resulted in exile from it is to understand, with the law of the esoteric, the secret of spiritual hermeneutics and, by that means, the secret of the spiritual history of man. It may be said that on this point the approach of Swedenborgian hermeneutics and that of Isma'ili hermeneutics are in profound accord. The Isma'ili authors emphasize repeatedly that when we practice *ta'wīl*, that is, the exegesis that "takes a thing back" to its hidden signification, to its esoteric, we in no way destroy the appearance that covers it, its exoteric. Just as we cannot see in this world, among humans, a spirit that does not subsist in a body, neither can we see an esoteric deprived of its exoteric appearance, or else it would no longer be the esoteric, that is, the internal content hidden under an appearance. When, therefore, the esoteric of Paradise is mentioned, there is no denial that there exists a garden of eternal delights, even if it is in the sense in which we see both Ṣadrā Shīrāzī and Swedenborg indicate how, in the other life, it is one or another form of spiritual consciousness that causes a manifestation of the substantial appearance (*apparentia realis*) which corresponds to it.[156]

Qāżī No'mān emphasizes this: "Understand this well, O group of faithful believers! . . . Let your hearts be perfectly conscious of it, for most of those among the men of this science [the men of *ta'wīl*, the esoterists] who go astray perish in this manner. It is also for this reason that Adam fell into the error in which he fell . . . For if the exoteric of a forbidden thing is a forbidden thing, its esoteric also corresponds to a forbidden thing; the esoteric does not transform the illicit into the licit, it cannot sanction libertinage. That is what must be known with regard to the exoteric and with regard to the esoteric."[157]

This is why all esoterists—a Swedenborg as well as those of Shi'ism and Isma'ilism—have seen here the secret of the human drama considered in its spiritual profundity. It is because there are two (complementary) ways of effecting an irreparable scission between the sensory and the spiritual, between the exoteric and the esoteric: namely, by an exclusive attachment to one or the other; the catastrophe is the same in either case. Esoterism degenerates into a purely abstract knowledge, that of the forces of nature, for example, or else succumbs to spiritual libertinage (whence the Shi'ite criticism of a certain type of Sufism); the exoteric, deprived of its theophanic function, degenerates into a covering, a hollow cortex, something like the corpse of what might have been an angelic appearance, if this would be conceivable. Everything, then, becomes institutionalized; dogmas are formulated; legalistic religion triumphs; the science of Nature becomes the conquest and possession of Nature, a science whose origin in the West is sometimes dated to the thirteenth century with Averroism, and which was abusively designated as "Arabism" because it was unknown that there was also in Islam the "prophetic philosophy" of Shi'ism. Certainly, once the mystical Sword of the Word is broken into pieces, nothing less than the *quest* of a Galahad is needed to reunite them. All the effort in the West from Robert Fludd to Goethe, from Boehme to Swedenborg, takes on this meaning, the meaning that is also that of the science of the alchemist Jābir ibn Ḥayyān for Isma'ili gnosis.[158]

Let us, then, consider the Garden of Eden. It does involve something that *is* a garden, but the hidden truth that *makes* a garden of it is found in its esoteric. Here, that esoteric is the divine inspiration (*ta'yīd*) that flows into the human being directly and without an intermediary, knowledge in the true sense, pure spiritual science in its subtle state. That is the garden whose sweetness surpasses all other sweetness; the one who understands this entirely renounces the interests of this world, because they have all become insipid for him, and consequently he is thenceforth bound to that spiritual knowledge and can only be one with it[159] (in Swedenborg, this is the state of the man of the *Antiquissima Ecclesia*). Showing him the garden, God says to Adam: "Dwell thou and thy wife in the Garden; and eat of the bountiful things therein as ye will; but approach not this tree, or ye run into harm and transgression" (Qur'ān 2:33). God puts them on their guard against Iblīs, who will not rest until he causes them to leave the garden (Qur'ān 20:115), that is, until he induces them to renounce the exoteric, which is, however, the "place" of the flowering of symbols.

Exoterically, in fact, the divine prohibition signifies that God opened to the human being all the esoteric ranks (*ḥodūd*) of the *da'wat*, that is, of the *Ecclesia spiritualis*; this determines the status for the entire time of our "cycle of occultation" as cycle of prophecy. This status is understood from a knowledge that has the exoteric, the *ẓāhir*, as a necessary intermediary, a knowledge that is thus essentially the perception of symbols, of the suprasensory concealed under this appearance, and which is concomitant with ritual obligations that are themselves invested with a symbolic signification. This is also the reason that something must remain inaccessible to man: the Tree that he is forbidden to profane. For Isma'ili gnosis, this Tree represents the Imām of the Resurrection (*Qā'im al-Qiyāmat*), the last Imām, whose future Appearance will conclude our cycle, will bring the time of our *Aiōn* to an end. He alone (who has been identified by many Twelve-Imām Shi'ite thinkers as the Paraclete, announced in the Gospel of John) will have the function of revealing the hidden sense of all Divine Revelations and of releasing men from their ritual obligations; what is today visible, exoteric (*ẓāhir*), will become hidden while what is today hidden, esoteric (*bāṭin*), will become manifest (in Isma'ili terms, this is the "seventh day" of Creation). That is why, by touching the forbidden Tree, the human being, the couple Adam-Eve, usurped the prerogative of the Resurrector; this means that he tried to do violence to the science of the Resurrection, which, until the coming of the last Imām, will remain inaccessible to man; in order to commit that violence, he had to break the union between the *ẓāhir* and the *bāṭin* that is presently necessary; or, rather, that breaking was itself his act of violence. In this way, man opened his own drama.[160]

Undoubtedly, he did this at the suggestion of Iblīs, whose intervention is explained better within the context of Isma'ili gnosis, since we already know about the previous existence of Iblīs and his intentions. In order for those intentions to succeed, Iblīs needed to awaken in man the nostalgia for that science of the Resurrection: "'Your Lord only forbade you this tree, lest ye should become angels or such beings as live forever.' And he swore to them both, that he was their sincere adviser" (Qur'ān 7:20-21). In fact, Iblīs and Adam had both belonged to the preceding "cycle of epiphany," where the "angelic" condition of man exempted him from the circuitousness of knowledge by means of symbols, as it exempted him from the obligations imposed by the enunciator-prophets (the *noṭaqā'*) of a religious Law (*sharī'at*). It is this memory that Iblīs awakens in Adam, in order to induce him to transgress the limit that marks the rank of the prophets, and to usurp the rank and the mission of the Imām of the Resurrection.[161]

This, then, is what unveils the profound sense of the simple words: "When they tasted of the tree, their shame [nudity] became manifest to them" (Qur'ān 7:22; see Gen. 3:7). It must be understood that the attempt on the part of man, Adam-Eve, to do away with the exoteric was equivalent to a laying bare of the esoteric (*bāṭin*), since it deprived the latter of its garment. As we have just mentioned, the esoteric in its pure state is the science that can only be manifested by the Imām of the Resurrection. Adam had neither the possibility nor the power. That is why, in wanting to lay bare the *bāṭin*, his own nakedness, that of Adam–Eve, was manifest to him, that is, his powerlessness, his ignorance, his internal darkness was laid bare (Swedenborg would say that it was the darkness of his *proprium*, his self, when this is separated from its Principle). Such is also the profound sense of this other qur'ānic verse: "Satan . . . stripped them of their raiment, to expose their shame" (7:27), that is, the raiment of the Divine Word, which, by means of its light (like a robe of light), concealed any darkness that might have been in them.

Adam and Eve together are the actors in this drama, since it destroys both the esoteric (Eve) and the exoteric (Adam). What happens, as we have said, is this: the desire, doomed to failure, to lay bare the esoteric prematurely has, as its corollary, the reduction of the exoteric from sensory appearance to the state of still life, to a corpse.[162] If a certain science of our time views Nature in this way, it may be said in return that it is this transgression which all esoterisms have subsequently tried to redeem, and that is their significance for a spiritual history invisible to historians of external events. However, because the triumph cannot occur except with the manifestation of the Imām-Paraclete, no esoterism, until the coming of the Imām, can be anything more than a *witness*, recognized by a small number, ridiculed by all the others, and not progressing except in the night of symbols.

The entire human drama is played out on the plane of gnosis and gnostic consciousness. It is a drama of knowledge, not a drama of the flesh. Our Isma'ili authors are the first to be amazed and indignant that the signification of the drama recounted in the Qur'ān and in the Bible could be degraded to the level of the common exegesis that we all know. They wonder about the reason for this: perhaps it is attributable, they think, to certain Jewish converts to Islam, who, unfortunately, were not esoterists. That exegesis has led to all sorts of puerile and unworthy explanations of the garment that Adam made for himself.[163] On the other hand, this is the spiritual sense that Isma'ili gnosis perceives in the verse: "They began to sew together the leaves of the Garden over their bodies" (Qur'ān 7:22; Gen. 3:7). Adam's attempt, we know, was equivalent to losing the sense of symbols; now, to lose the sense of symbols is to be placed in the presence of his own darkness, his own ignorance, it is to see his own nakedness. Both Adam and Eve, then, frustrated in their endeavor for a pure esoteric (*bāṭin*) that inevitably escapes them, become attached to ***remembrance***, as to the last light of wisdom. This remembrance of lost symbols constitutes the "leaves of the Garden" by means of which they try to ***veil*** their state, the nakedness that was ***unveiled*** to them by the fact that divine inspiration (*ta'yīd*) was withdrawn from them. Have men been doing anything else since then? As Qāżī No'mān remarks, many have perished in this effort, by misjudging its finality or by succumbing to spiritual libertinage.[164]

Nevertheless, the end of the episode, in both the qur'ānic teaching and in Isma'ili hermeneutics, has none of the somber resonance to which the religious man of the West has become accustomed over the centuries. It is said that Adam did not persist in his error and that God returned to him, for He is "Oft-returning [*al-Tawwab*], most Merciful" (Qur'ān 2:37).[165] Adam departed from Paradise, but thenceforth, by means of gnosis, he effected a return to the "potential paradise" which is the ***da'wat***. The qur'ānic verses say this: "Their Lord called unto them: 'Did I not forbid you that tree [that is, the science of the Resurrection], and tell you that Satan was an avowed enemy unto you? . . . Get ye down with enmity between yourselves [Adam and Satan]. On earth will be your dwelling place and your means of livelihood,—for a time . . . but from it shall ye be taken out [at last]'" (7:22, 24, 25).

The call that God addresses to them is not, of course, that of a voice that makes the air vibrate physically; it is the reuniting of spiritual science to their consciousness. For when God "returns" to them, He does not degrade Adam from the rank of the caliphate and the Imāmate that He had established for him; He does not deprive him completely of His Word, of His wisdom—

in brief, of that divine vitality (*māddat*) that is the "column of light," divine magnetism, gnosis.[166] But He causes him to "descend" from Paradise, that is, from the "celestial" state that is the *ta'wīl* without its veil, the direct and immediate spiritual perception of the esoteric sense, of the symbolism of beings and things. He causes him to descend "to earth," the earth that is the *da'wat*, the Isma'ili sodality, where the "primordial divine vitality" is conjoined to the initiates, but only by means of the intermediary of all the ranks of the celestial and earthly hierarchies.[167] It is this "spiritual earth" of the *da'wat* that is their temporary abode, while they wait for the "seventh day" to dawn,[168] and that is why he who responds to the Call, to the *da'wat*, has thenceforth returned virtually to Paradise. It is this "virtual paradise" of which, in the period of Noah, the Ark is the symbol; in it are grouped the Friends of God and their adherents, and the "party of Iblīs," to use the qur'ānic expression, is the party of those whom Iblīs had taken possession of to the point of making them forget the remembrance (*dhikr*) of God. There is another profound note here: this "forgetfulness" is their "delay" (*ta'khīr*); now, we know that Isma'ili metaphysics understands the origin of *time* as a "delay of eternity" that occurred "in Heaven."[169]

The work of Iblīs becomes worse throughout the period of Adam, a period that is given its rhythm by the succession of Imāms who were the posterity of Seth, son and Imām of Adam, to whom Adam confided his secret. Their names correspond to the names that we can read in the fifth chapter of the book of Genesis,[170] and their line leads us to the arising of a new prophet, Noah, who opens a new period of prophecy, necessitated by the increasing corruption of the posterity of Adam.

3. The Esoteric Sense of the History of Noah

Noah is the second day of hierohistory, that is, of the *hexaēmeron*, the six days of spiritual Creation that must lead to the manifestation of the Perfect Man, to the "seventh day" that concludes our *Aiōn*, in the person of the last Imām, who announces the Resurrection of Resurrections (*Qiyāmat al-Qiyāmāt*). While the Qur'ān, in accord with the Bible, numbers the "duration of Noah" at 950 years, our Isma'ili authors know very well that this impressive number of years relates not to the age of Noah the individual and his physical person, but to the duration of his period in the cycle of prophecy[171] (in the same way, as we have seen, Swedenborg relates this figure to the duration of the *Antiqua Ecclesia*). In the events that filled this period in the history of prophecy, Isma'ili gnosis discerns the same number of spiritual events; everything is transposed to the initiatory plane, resulting, of course, not in a succession of allegories, but in a succession of real events, "coded" under the appearance of external events, a secret history remaining unknown to those who are attached only to the latter. It is impossible for us to analyze in detail the sequence of these events; we can only emphasize the symbols typical of the qur'ānic and biblical history of Noah.

In order to orientate our attention, let us recall that these symbols are essentially the event of the *Flood* and the construction and navigation of the *Ark*. On these two points we will encounter, in relation to Swedenborg's hermeneutics, a convergence that seems to presage the fruits that may be expected from a comparative study in depth of the spiritual hermeneutics of the Bible and the Qur'ān. Here again, the Flood is a spiritual event, a real event that takes place in souls, a *suffocation* of souls as a consequence of the same drama of Knowledge opened by Adam at the beginning of his cycle. The motive forces of the drama are designated as the exoteric and the esoteric of the Divine Word; the *dramatis personae* are determined by the role and attitude that people assume, respectively, toward the exoteric and the esoteric. In this way most of humanity will be drowned and suffocated by the exoteric of the Divine Revelations, the literal appearance of positive religion, either because some do not want to know anything more than the exoteric, or because others assert that they do not need anything more. Both, for opposite but complementary reasons, will refuse to take a place in the *Ark*, the symbolic signification of which is self-evident.

The figure of Noah belongs to the category of prophet-messengers (*Nabī Morsal, Nabī* and *Rasūl*),[172] instructed to set out to man a new religious Law, a new *sharī'at*. Now, as such, as the mission of an Enunciator-Prophet (*Nāṭiq*), Noah's mission essentially consists in calling people to the *ẓāhir*, to the exoteric and, by this means, to the observance of ritual. His call is accepted only by those who have a modest enough opinion of themselves to understand this necessity, and they are a small minority. On the other hand, Noah's preaching instantly unites against him, in the posterity of Iblīs, a double opposition: those who consider that they can and must have immediate access to the esoteric, to the *bāṭin*; and those who are the prey of the exoteric left to itself, as we have seen, as a result of Adam's transgression, and who reject any esoteric implication. Thus, the leaders object to Noah: "We see in thee nothing but a man like ourselves" (Qur'ān 11:27). In other words, Noah is not bringing them anything new; the exoteric is something that everyone already knows, and the only advantage that it has for them is to permit them to satisfy their will to power through keeping people together by agreement or by force. That is why, in order to divert their people from Noah's preaching, they say to them: "Abandon not your gods" (Qur'ān 71:23), that is, the learned from whom they had received teaching until then, those learned in the Law, who were only masters in misleading them (71:24).[173]

From that moment, Noah knows, by divine inspiration, that the number of his adherents will not increase, and the same divine inspiration orders him to construct the Ark (Qur'ān 11:36 ff.). Let us note here again the importance that our authors attach to the simultaneous preservation of the *ẓāhir* and the *bāṭin*, the symbol and the symbolized. The image of the Ark is an image that is absolutely necessary in order that the sense of the *da'wat*, the Isma'ili Convocation, may appear before the spiritual catastrophe already begun. To construct the Ark is, at God's order, to establish the *da'wat*, the esoteric sodality together with its grades and its initiation, so that the spirits of its adherents may find, through the life of the spiritual science that is imbued with the nature of light (*ḥayāt al-'ilm al-rūḥānī al-nūrānī*), salvation outside of submersion in unconsciousness, outside of negation and misleading, just as a ship preserves bodies from drowning in the physical sense.[174] In the face of this effort, the leaders of Noah's people act as their sort has always acted in relation to the gnostics: "Every time that the Chiefs of his people passed by him," the qur'ānic verse tells us, "they threw ridicule on him. He said: 'If ye ridicule us now, we [in our turn] can look down on you with ridicule likewise! But soon will ye know who it is on whom will descend a penalty that will cover them with shame,—on whom will be unloosed a penalty lasting'" (11:38-39).

We are reminded that Water is the symbol of knowledge and of everything that relates to it; each, respectively, the symbol and the symbolized (each at its own level of being is the symbol of the other), can either safeguard life or cause death. Those who are conveyed by a secure ark float safe and sound from the peril of the water; those who have a rank in the *da'wat* float safe and sound on the ocean of knowledge. Thus, there is a perfect correspondence between every detail of the structure of the Ark and the structure of the *da'wat*. It is impossible to enter into these details here. Without difficulty, Qāżī No'mān indicates how the structure of the Ark permits a reference to be read in it to the *four*, to the *seven*, and to the *twelve*: to the *four* figures that dominate respectively the celestial hierarchy (First Intelligence and First Soul, *Sābiq* and *Tālī*) and the earthly hierarchy (Prophet and Imām); to the *seven* prophets of the cycle (that is, including the Imām of the Resurrection, the "seventh day")[175] and to the *seven* Imāms of each period; and to the *twelve Ḥojjat* who permanently surround every Imām of every period.[176] Each of these correspondences also emphasizes the permanence of the symbol of the eternal *da'wat*, from period to period in the cycle of prophecy, for all these correspondences are found as well in the symbol of the Christian cross with its four branches and in the structure of the *shahādat*, the testimony of the Unique for the Islamic faith (four words, seven syllables, twelve letters). Exoterically, these symbols may differ among themselves; esoterically, our author stresses, the archetype (the *aṣl*) remains the same.

The establishment of a *da'wat* appropriate to its period, that is, the construction of the Ark by Noah, is therefore the Call, the *da'wat*, inviting men to take their place in the Ark, in the ranks of the higher spiritual science. Of course, the lack of success is as complete as it was before, when Noah called men only to the exoteric. It is this failure that is recorded in a prayer of Noah, reported in moving terms in the qur'ānic verses: "O my Lord! I have called to my people *night and day*, but my call only increases their flight. And every time I have called to them, that Thou mightest forgive them, they have only *thrust their fingers into their ears*, covered themselves up with their garments, grown obstinate, and given themselves up to arrogance. So I have called to them aloud; further I have spoken to them *in public* and *secretly in private*, saying, 'Ask forgiveness from your Lord; for He is *Oft-Forgiving*; He will *send rain* (*from Heaven*) to you in abundance; give you increase in *wealth* and in *sons*; and bestow on you *gardens* and bestow on you *rivers of flowing water*'" (71:5-12). Let us consider with Qāżī No'mān the esoteric sense of these verses (in which we have italicized here the symbolic words); we will discover, along with the sense of the hierohistory of Noah, the actual sense of what is designated by the name of the Flood.

A Call made *day and night*; a Call made *openly*, which is followed by *secret* conversations: this signifies Noah's double Call, calling to the *exoteric* as Enunciator-Prophet of a *sharī'at*, and calling to the *esoteric*, that is, to the *da'wat*, to the mystic sodality that he established in the person of his Imām as a repository of the secret of his preaching, and by his Imām in the person of all those who took their place, according to their rank, in the

Ark. All the prophets have done this (it is easily grasped how all this tends to restore order to things out of balance—out of balance originally because of Adam's transgression). The word *forgiveness* (*ghofrān*), even in its etymology ("act of veiling"), indicates to us what must be understood each time we encounter it: to ask divine "forgiveness" is to enter into the esoteric of the *da'wat*. That God loves to forgive means that He loves to confer upon us the gift of esoteric knowledge.[177] *Heaven* symbolizes with the Enunciator-Prophet (*Nāṭiq*) as the Heaven that dominates the *mesocosm* (or *hierocosmos, 'ālam al-Dīn*), the hieratic world intermediate between the macrocosm and the microcosm. Therefore, when you have asked for the gift of esoteric spiritual science, God rains down Knowledge, true *wealth*, upon you from the Heaven of prophecy; He gives you increase in *sons*, that is, you in turn will be Callers (*dā'ī*) to whom men will respond (*mostajībūn*, your spiritual sons). We know that the promised *gardens* are the symbol of the *da'wat* (potential paradise), vivified by those *rivers of flowing water* that are the gnostics who compose the *Ecclesia spiritualis*. But it is this Call of Noah that the chiefs and the learned in Law ridiculed with their mockery (Qur'an 11:38).

From that point, there is a presentiment as to what the Flood will consist in as a spiritual event, something much graver than the geological catastrophe, the physical phenomenon that is its symbol. On one hand, it will result in the Water "that flows from the Heaven of prophecy," and on the other hand, following the letter of the qur'ānic verse (11:40), in the boiling over or gushing forth from the mysterious furnace called *al-tannūr* (it is known that the furnace of the European alchemists was designated by the word *atanor*, transcribed from Arabic). This coming to boiling signifies, acording to Qāżī No'mān, the advent of the *ta'wīl*, that is, of the esoteric hermeneutics that dispense light, offered by the one whom Noah instituted as his Imām, the repository of his secret. From that point also, the Water appears in its ambivalent symbolism. For those who have "entered into the Ark," it is the Water that bears them; for those who have refused, it is the Water that suffocates them, the unconsciousness whose monstrous waves the Ark must cleave.[178]

"Those who have entered into the Ark" are all those to whom the divine order has referred: "We said: 'Embark therein, of each kind two, male and female'" (Qur'ān 11:40), for this order concerns the *da'wat*, the Isma'ili sodality. The degrees of its esoteric hierarchy form couples among themselves: each grade (*ḥadd*, "limit") forms a couple with the grade that comes immediately after it (*maḥdūd*, that which is "limited" by it) and that it carries along behind it, all being responsible for each other until the Afterlife.[179] Moreover, each grade of the earthly hierarchy forms a couple with the grade that corresponds to it in the celestial hierarchy.[180] Therefore, it is to all the members of the mystic brotherhood that Noah addresses himself when he says: "Embark ye on the Ark, in the name of God, whether it move or be at rest!" (11:41).

"So the Ark floated with them on the waves [towering] like mountains" (11:42), which means: the Imām, invested with esoteric teaching, floats in his *da'wat* like a mystical Ark, together with all those who have responded to his Call (the *mostajībūn*), on the ocean of knowledge; he floats from mystical grade to grade (from *ḥadd* to *ḥadd*), in order to initiate each one into the higher spiritual science (*ma'rifat*); the waves that he confronts, towering like mountains, are the learned in Law, the literalists (*'ulamā' al-ẓāhir*) who pass as men of science, although they are empty of any knowledge in the true sense; that is why they collapse before the Imām, as the waves of the sea collapse after having given the illusion of being high mountains. "The divine *da'wat* (the mystical Ark) floats upon the heads of these people who give themselves the airs of the learned. It cleaves them as a ship cleaves the waves. It floats upon them while they frighten men with their shallow science, inflating themselves in the way that the waves of the sea rise and collide with each other . . . . But those who have entered the *da'wat* are sheltered there from their misleading, as the traveler in a ship is sheltered from the waves."[181]

Among the latter, alas, one of the sons of Noah is absent; the Qur'ān alludes to his case, and Isma'ili hermeneutics clarifies the meaning of his transgression. That transgression is nothing other than a repetition of the attitude of Iblīs with regard to Adam. Noah calls him: "O my son! Embark with us, and be not with the unbelievers" (11:42). In vain. His son had hoped that the Imāmate would be conferred upon him. Frustrated in his hope, like Iblīs, he prefers to take refuge alone on a high mountain. Perhaps the latter also symbolizes, as Qāẑī No'mān says, the learned in Law, the literalists, since it is true that the hero of a "failed initiation" has no other refuge than agnosticism, whether it is that of the pious literalists or that of the desperate. Noah intercedes for him in vain. He is told in response: "O Noah! he is not of thy family" (11:46), that is, of your spiritual family, the mystical companions of the Ark. That is why "the waves came between them, and the son was among those overwhelmed in the Flood" (11:43), overwhelmed by doubts, uncertainties, and the false knowledge that destroys the symbols by isolating the symbol (the *ẓāhir*) from the symbolized (the *bāṭin*).[182]

Although we are summarizing here in bold outline, something can be glimpsed. The spiritual truth of the phenomenon "Flood," the reality of the event as it occurs in the esoteric, that is, in souls, is seen to be similar as it is brought out by the spiritual hermeneutics of Swedenborg on one hand, and by Isma'ili hermeneutics on the other. This acknowledgment is important for our subject of a comparative study of spiritual hermeneutics. We have read in Swedenborg that, from one aspect, the Flood was the suffocation of men by spiritual things for which, once deprived of their internal respiration, they no longer had an organ. In Isma'ili gnosis, in the person of the leaders and in that of Noah's son, who recapitulates the pretension of Iblīs, we see man frustrated, as Adam was after having yielded to the suggestion of

Iblīs, and suffocating in his inability to achieve an esoteric stripped of its covering. From another aspect (the two aspects being complementary), we have read in Swedenborg how the absence of spiritual things that had been the "breath of his life" for man caused in him the suffocation and death of his spiritual organism. In Isma'ili gnosis this corresponds to the suffocation produced by the science of the pure exoterists, the learned in Law, who want to know only the appearance, the actual letter, without any signification that goes beyond it. The two complementary aspects correspond to the ambivalence of the symbolism of Water: the Water which is the knowledge that gives life, and which may become the knowledge that suffocates and causes death, if refuge is not taken in the Ark.

This convergence of our spiritual hermeneutics is also felt in the meaning that they bring out with regard to the departure from the Ark. The end of the Flood is signified by the order that is recounted by the qur'ānic verse: "Then the word went forth: 'O earth! swallow up thy water, and O sky! withhold [thy rain]!'" (11:44). It is the entire future of the esoteric *da'wat* that is signified here. We know that the Sky [Heaven] is the symbol of the prophet (and the reverse). Noah had received the order to call men to the exoteric, to the observance of the *sharī'at* set out by him, and also to call them to the esoteric, to the secret and purely spiritual sense of that *sharī'at*, that is, to enter into the mystical Ark. From that time on, each prophet will limit himself strictly to his role as Enunciator of a *sharī'at*: he will only call men to strict ritual observance. "O earth! swallow up thy water" means that spiritual science—the Water that gushed forth from the esoteric Earth that is the Imāmate, at the same time that the Water flowed from the Heaven of prophecy—will henceforth withdraw into the person of the Imām as the abode of the esoteric.[183] As the waters vanish from sight when they are absorbed by the earth, so secret gnosis withdraws and remains hidden in the person of the one who is its abode. This is the last resting place of the Ark. The Qur'ān mentions not Ararat, but another name. "The Ark rested on Mount Jūdī" (11:44), and this final point designates the last degree, or, rather, in the order of initiation, the initial degree of the esoteric hierarchy, that of the neophytes (the ***mostajībūn***). We have read, in fact, that the mystical Ark (esoteric science) floats, together with the Imām, from grade to grade in the entire hierarchy. It finally comes to rest on the last, the initial grade, below which there is only the profane world, that is, the exoterists.[184] To them, nothing will be unveiled, except to the elect, who, one by one, will respond to the ***daʿwat***, to the "calling" secretly addressed to them by the Imām.

"The word came: 'O Noah! come down from the Ark with peace from Us and blessing on thee and on some of the peoples [who will spring] from those with thee'" (Qur'ān 11:48). Swedenborgian hermeneutics has shown us that the command "Go forth from the Ark" puts an end to the ordeal of the "Flood" for those who have overcome it victoriously and have thus become spiritually free men (see supra § 6). Similarly, for Isma'ili gnosis, the sojourn in the Ark has the sense of an ordeal: those who have passed through it become true believers in the invisible world (***mu'minīn fī'l-ghayb***).[185] All the others are those who "remain delayed" (***takhalluf***)[186] with respect to the spiritual or gnostic realities of faith (***ḥaqā'iq al-īmān***), consequently those who violate the pact of faith in the invisible (***al-īmān bi'l-ghayb***), those who establish the exoteric independently of the esoteric (***iqāmat al-ẓāhir dūna'l-bāṭin***), and who do not admit that there is celestial support for theosophical wisdom (***al-ta'yīd bi'l-ḥikmat***), for secret spiritual gnosis (***ʿilm maknūn rūḥānī maṣūn***).[187] The final prayer of Noah (Qur'ān 71:26-27) asks God to preserve his ***daʿwat*** from their incursion and from their corrupting nature.[188] Noah may depart from the Ark because it has now come to rest at a final point; the Waters (esoteric gnosis) have withdrawn and hidden themselves in the Imām and his own. All those whom the Ark has preserved move around incognito and free among men, the masses who are incapable of enduring the encounter between the celestial Waters and the Waters that gush forth from the Earth, that is, between the science of the exoteric (that of the prophets) and the science of the esoteric (that of the Imāms).[189] The departure from the Ark is accompanied by the discipline of the ***arcanum***. It will remain so until the advent of the last Imām, the Imām of the Resurrection, who alone will have the function of revealing openly the *ta'wīl*, the concealed sense of all Divine Revelations.[190]

It is on the perspective of this prophetic succession that the Isma'ili chapter of the spiritual history of Noah ends, with regard to these qur'ānic verses: "And We sent Noah and Abraham, and established in their line Prophethood and Revelation [the Book]. . . . Then, in their wake, we followed them up [others of] Our apostles: We sent after them Jesus the son of Mary, and bestowed on him the Gospel" (57:26-27).

These qur'ānic verses, together with several others, best express the theme that, in Islamic prophetology (actually, Shi'ite prophetology), echoes the theme of *Verus Propheta* in primitive Judeo-Christian theology: the *True Prophet*, hastening from prophet to prophet until the place of his rest, the last prophet. The purest substance of prophecy will be transferred from Adam to one descendant after another, until Noah; from him, until Moses; from Moses, until Jesus; from Jesus, until Muḥammad. It is not only a matter of physical posterity, since neither Moses nor Jesus had any, but also of spiritual posterity and descent by birth in the *da'wat* (*bi-mawlid al-da'wat*).[191] However, Shi'ite prophetology contains something more than Judeo-Christian prophetology, something that is already promised in the juxtaposition emphasized in the verse cited above: ***prophecy and the Book***. For Shi'ite prophetology, the Book, in esoteric terms, designates the Imām, since in its integrality the "phenomenon of the Sacred Book" presupposes not only the enunciation of the exoteric letter by the prophet but also the spiritual science of the esoteric that has its foundation in the Imām. The prophetic succession, in both the Isma'ili and the Twelve-Imām Shi'ite conception, includes simultaneously the line of the great prophets (the "law-giving" prophets) and the line of their Imāms.

There is here a fact of major importance for the actual concept of a "spiritual line." In fact, if the Shi'ites find expressly affirmed in the Qur'ān the Abrahamic descent of Jesus, this can only mean a spiritual descent, since Jesus did not have an "earthly" father, a father of the flesh. On the other hand, we know that since the hierohistory of Adam the esoteric is the Feminine (and the reverse). From this stems the typological correspondence that Shi'ite thought establishes between Maryam, mother of Jesus, and Fāṭima, daughter of the Prophet Muḥammad and mother of the holy Imāms, a correspondence that is so striking and of such still unsuspected implication. Shi'ism generally is sometimes reproached for basing the principle of prophetic succession on the idea of physical descent. It is simply forgotten that this kind of descent has never sufficed: both *naṣṣ* and *'iṣmat*, investiture and complete purity, are also necessary. It is also forgotten that physical descent is through the feminine, in the person of Fāṭima, daughter of the Prophet Muḥammad, which would be sufficient to place the line of Imāms outside of any comparison with some political dynasty, "legitimate" or not. In a moving conversation with the Abbasid caliph of Baghdad, the Seventh Imām of the Shi'ites, Mūsā Kāẓem (d. 183/799), responded pertinently by emphasizing the typological correspondence between Maryam and Fāṭima: just as Jesus possesses his prophetic ancestry from a woman, Maryam, so do the Imāms possess their prophetic ancestry from their mother, Fāṭima.[192]

The implication of this parallelism is understood perfectly only if it is known that the Feminine represents the esoteric. Isma'ili Christology will indicate to us that it is actually this which gives its meaning to the "virginal conception" of Jesus, and all of Shi'ite theology extends the qualification of Virgin Mother to the person of Fāṭima (*al-Batūl*). This is what shows through the meaning that Christianity takes on in the comprehensive conception of unitary prophetic religion as embracing the entire history of humanity. Adam's transgression consisted in yielding to the suggestion of Iblīs: to attain to the esoteric in its pure state. Christianity will be understood here as originating in the purely esoteric, in the secret of the "virginal conception" of its prophet, while Shi'ism, as the esoterism of Islam, claims a corresponding ancestry. It may, therefore, be said that what is proclaimed in the typological correspondence between Maryam and Fāṭima is the final advent of the Imām-Paraclete, with which all the consequences of Adam's transgression will be abolished, because by revealing the esoteric of all Divine Revelations, he will reveal the secret of the Resurrection.

What, then, can be said of Shi'ite Christology in general and more specifically of Isma'ili Christology? The question is of great importance, since all research in depth on comparative spiritual hermeneutics of the Bible and the Qur'ān will conclude, at one time or another, by encountering the Christological differences. Shi'ite prophetology is completely comfortable in conceiving a Christology, and it has done so. On the other hand, it has been impossible until now for Christian Christology, at least in its official form, to conceive of a prophetology capable of evaluating positively the significance of the Muḥammadan prophetic revelation. Because the "history of religions" has continued subsequently to Christianity, we are faced with a *fundamental problem* in the spiritual history of man, a problem that is undoubtedly insurmountable for some and stimulating for others; in any case it is one that has been very little reflected upon, and that remains posed in all its theological extent, because every political philosophy in history in fact bypasses the problem that is actually posed. Of course, the data vary according to the form of the Christology itself, and there has been a certain amount of data in Christianity outside the official Christology of the Councils. It is certain, for example, that in the theology of Swedenborg, which does not accept the idea of the Trinity—at least as official dogma accepts it—Christology takes on an entirely different form. We do not have the time or the space here to refer to it for our project of comparative spiritual hermeneutics, but we can indicate provisionally the broad outline of the Christology of Isma'ili gnosis, and discern the perspective toward which it orientates us.

4. *Isma'ili Christology*

We will discuss this subject only allusively and in a few lines, referring to the work of Qāżī No'mān, but without following in detail the Isma'ili exegesis of the qur'ānic verses cited, as this would require lengthy treatment. Let us remind ourselves that here again the *ta'wīl*, Isma'ili hermeneutics, transposes all the events onto the spiritual or initiatory plane, on the basis of a doctrine of correspondences that has never been found—and never can be found—in that false situation, that impasse, in the face of which certain theologians of our time have spoken of the need to "demythologize" the data of biblical history. Far from it. For the most part, we can identify in the canonical Gospels or in the Gospels that are considered apocryphal the sources of the Christology that is related in the qur'ānic verses or the *ḥadīth* (the traditions of the Prophet Muḥammad) that are referred to by the Shi'ite and Isma'ili theosophers. The reflections of these men result in a gnostic exegesis of the sources that is completely unexpected given our habits of thought.

The chapter that expounds the *ta'wīl*, the spiritual interpretation of the history of Jesus, or his hierohistory, is prefaced with a chapter that begins by giving the Isma'ili gnostic interpretation of the history of Zacharias.[193] The discussion here involves, as it does from one end to the other of the cycle of prophecy, the hierohistory of the *da'wat*, and *eo ipso* the spiritual history of humanity; the *dramatis personae* will again be the "dignitaries" of the eternal *da'wat*, "in Heaven" and on earth. Their decisions and their behavior have no meaning except in relation to the hierohistory of that eternal *da'wat*, and something results from this that has no analogy, as far as I know, in any other gnosis.

Let us bear in mind the process of the double prophetic and imāmic succession. The mission of the Prophet-Messenger (*Nabī-Morsal*) is to enunciate, to reveal the exoteric of a new religious Law. Beside him, he whom he establishes as his Imām is simultaneously the treasurer ***and*** the treasure of the esoteric of the positive religion. As long as the Enunciator-Prophet (*Nāṭiq*) is in this world, the Imām is the Silent One (*ṣāmit*). For the prophet, he is the preeminent *Ḥojjat* (his Proof, his Pledge). Esoterically, the Imām, since he is invested with the esoteric, is the Enunciator of the Law in relation to the prophet, as the feminine in relation to the masculine; we noted above that the Imām is therefore designated as the "spiritual mother" of the believers (in Persian *mādar-e rūḥānī*). When the Prophet leaves this world, the Imām succeeds him at the head of the community and assumes his "masculine" spiritual responsibilities. From among the twelve permanent *Ḥojjat*, he chooses one who will then, in his turn, be at his side in the role that he himself played at the side of the Prophet, by assuming the "feminine" esoteric. The Imām-*Ḥojjat* couple succeeds the Prophet-Imām couple. When the Imām disappears, the *Ḥojjat*, in turn, succeeds him, and so forth. The promotion of a *Ḥojjat* results from the spiritual conjunction of the prophetic-masculine (the prophet or the Imām who succeeds him) and the esoteric-feminine (the Imām for the prophet, the *Ḥojjat* for the Imām). This is the norm of succession and regular initiatory filiation that must be kept in mind in order to understand the figure of Maryam, mother of Jesus.

When the fourth period of the cycle of prophecy, that is, the period of Moses, was in the process of reaching its end, the Imām of the time was named 'Imrān.[194] He had the foreknowledge that he would not live until the fifth great prophet would be raised up (that is, Jesus, prophet of the "fifth day" of the *hexaēmeron*). His own *Ḥojjat* had left this world before they had been able, together, to choose the one who would have been the future Imām, the spiritual successor of 'Imrān, spiritually born (*wilādat rūḥānīya*), so to speak, of the latter and his *Hojjat*. That is why 'Imrān had designated Zacharias in advance as the Imām, his successor. But Zacharias did not belong directly to the *da'wat* of 'Imrān, that is, to his *jazīra*, those who owed their initiatory birth directly to 'Imrān. In order to provide for the future, 'Imrān also chose from among his young dignitaries the one in whom he discerned the greatest spiritual precociousness, and he entrusted him to Zacharias for his initiatory education, so that the young man could eventually succeed Zacharias one day and return the imāmic succession to the spiritual line of 'Imrān. The young disciple whom 'Imrān entrusted to the care of Zacharias was designated exoterically by the name Maryam.[195]

In fact, Maryam was shown not to have the aptitude for the Imāmate, but, rather, to have the aptitude for the function of *Ḥojjat*, that is, as being devoted essentially to the esoteric, as a figure who is, esoterically, "in the essential feminine," so that 'Imrān's hope was fulfilled, but in a way that he had not foreseen. We find ourselves here simultaneously before the mystery of the figure of Maryam and before the rigorous implications of Isma'ili gnosis. For the name Maryam can also conceal a dignitary of the *da'wat* who would be physically masculine, a man. In fact, grammatically, our text passes with indifference from the masculine to the feminine and vice versa. Since the beginning of the history of Adam-Eve, we know that the esoteric is essentially the feminine. Whether the figure of Maryam is physically—legally, so to speak—a man or a woman is not important; what is important is the metaphysical and esoteric status, which, in terms of its rank and status in the *da'wat*, is essentially the feminine. Thus, regardless of whether he is physically a man, his real status is the same. Certain historical examples, however, indicate that this figure could also be physically a woman who assumes the spiritual role of a man in the feminine.[196] That is why he is spoken of in the feminine, and the case of Maryam is repeated typologically with regard to all the feminine names of hierohistory

(Khadīja, wife of the Prophet Muḥammad, Fāṭima, his daughter, Mary Magdalene as another name for Simon Peter, etc.).[197] From this will follow the meaning of the initiatives taken by Maryam, which lead, under the direction of the *celestial ḥodūd*, to the raising up of the new prophet.

For his part, Zacharias felt the desire to ensure the imāmic succession in its proper spiritual descent. With the help of his *Ḥojjat* (corresponding to the figure of Elisabeth), he was able to establish, belatedly, it is true, Yaḥyā, that is, John the Baptist, as his future successor. Yaḥyā would be Imām for a while after Zacharias, but he would not be of his succession as Zacharias had arranged it. In the meantime, the spiritual education of Maryam goes forward; in fact, Zacharias does not play much of a role in this, for Maryam receives everything not from a human master, but from invisible celestial Guides (the qur'ānic verse 3:37 alludes to this: each time that Zacharias enters Maryam's room, he discovers that she is already provided with a mysterious food). This is the situation until the scene of the Annunciation, which the Qur'ān divides into two parts. First the Angels (the celestial "dignitaries" whose hierarchy corresponds to the ranks of the earthly *da'wat*) announce the figure of Jesus to Mary: his name, the discourses that he will give, and the works that he will accomplish. Then, there is the personal manifestation of the Angel Gabriel as Holy Spirit.

In order to make us understand the meaning of these events on the initiatory plane, Qāżī No'mān explains: Maryam as *Ḥojjat*, as a feminine figure symbolizing the pure esoteric, is not qualified to receive the solemn obligation that integrates a new initiate into the *da'wat*; she cannot do this except with the consent and spiritual assistance of the Imām, who, as the successor of the prophet of the period, symbolizes esoterically the "masculine," the "spiritual father." This is the reason for Maryam's fear and protestations at the Annunciation of the Angel. She asks the Angel to swear before God that he is not of those whom the discipline of the *arcanum* (*taqīyeh*) would forbid having such a purpose, which would reult in violating the solemn pact that pledges them to the Imām. According to the exoteric letter of the qur'ānic text, she protests that she is not a "woman of wicked life"; this means that she has never infringed the mystical law of the sodality by denying the role and the prerogative of the Imām: "'How shall I have a son, seeing that no man has touched me?'" (Qur'ān 19:20; cf. Luke 1:34).

In fact, at first sight, and as Isma'ili hermeneutics reads the text, what the Angel announces to Maryam can only appear to her as an enormity. By ordering her to receive the entry of Jesus in the *da'wat* (to "give him birth" in the *da'wat*), he instructs her, by God's command, to receive, without the knowledge, order, or consent of the Imām, not simply the entry of a young man as a new initiate, but the entry of one who will be the future prophet, the prophet of the "fifth day" of spiritual Creation, that is, of the fifth period in the cycle of prophecy; and this prophet will be "her son" in the higher spiritual and esoteric signification of the word, "Jesus son of Maryam." The appearance of the Angel signifies the conjunction—immediate and without intermediary—with Maryam of what the Isma'ili lexicon designates as *ta'yīd*, celestial aid, as *māddat*, pre-eternal vivifying and fecundating divine vitality, "column of light," divine magnetism, etc.[198] The law of regular initiatory filiation, and thus the earthly lineage of the prophetic succession, insofar as it is earthly, is broken by the direct celestial intervention of the Angel. The mystery of the "virginal conception" of Christ is here; it is not something that belongs to the physical nature of the human body; it is the "spiritual birth" of the future prophet as proceeding, by the command of Heaven, uniquely from his mother, that is, from the purely esoteric, without intervention of the masculine principle that is the exoteric and the Law. This is not a question of allegory; the *spiritual truth* of the event, recaptured on the plane to which it relates, is the *literal truth.* Isma'ili gnosis thus gives the origins of Christianity and its function in human history the meaning that integrates it into the eternal *da'wat.*

Certainly, this is a Christianity altogether different from the one generally studied in the official history of external events; but there are perhaps traces of this "other Christianity" to be found in certain Western traditions. The sequence of spiritual events is rigorously connected according to Isma'ili hermeneutics. When the moment arrives, the Imām of the time, John the Baptist (Yaḥyā), son of Zacharias, is the first to approve the initiative taken by Maryam at the Angel's order, and to bow before the new prophet. This is the scene of the Baptism of Christ, reported in our canonical Gospels and recorded in many *ḥadīth*, through which our Isma'ili authors know about it, but they give it a meaning that converges with the one given to it in other respects by Judeo-Christian gnosis. Finally, the Qur'ān (4:157) is resolutely "docetist": Christ did not die on the cross; God raised him up unto Himself, for men did not have the power to kill the Word of God (*Kalām Allāh*), the Spirit of God (*Rūḥ Allāh*). But men had the illusion that they killed him, and in doing so they obtained what they wanted: doubt, perplexity, misleading (all that we call "agnosticism"); the "punishment" that is promised to them is exactly this. On the other hand, the mysterious meal to which certain qur'ānic verses allude (5:115-118) is interpreted by our Isma'ili authors as a mystical Communion, as the form of Manifestation assumed by Jesus after his disappearance in order to give his teaching to his disciples; and this, Qāẓī No'mān emphasizes, is not reported of any other prophet. Henceforth, all the Shi'ite traditions say, Christ will not "reappear" except when the Imām of the Resurrection (the *Qā'im al-Qiyāmat*) will himself appear, and will have scattered before him all the deniers.

The Isma'ili chapter of the spiritual history of Jesus closes with an allusion to the meaning that must be given to the instruction ordering everyone "to take up his Cross."[199] The symbol of the Cross, not in the sense that is familiar to Christian asceticism, but in its internal esoteric reality, involves the same significations as the Ark constructed by Noah and the four words that compose the *shahādat*, the Islamic testimony of Unity. The symbol of the Christian Cross, thus integrated into the hierohistory of the eternal and unique *da'wat*, addresses to believers the same Call to faith and to a return to the suprasensory spiritual world, a Call that makes known to them its presence by unveiling for them the correspondences of universes that symbolize with each other. This Call may differ as far as exoteric aspects are concerned, but the spiritual hermeneutics of the prophets' teaching, from one end of the cycle of earthly humanity to the other, preserves its unity. For esoterism, everywhere and always, leads to the same end.

We mentioned a little while ago that perhaps the most dramatic problem in discussing the spiritual history of man results from the stop arbitrarily imposed on this history, when theologies claim to impose limits upon the God Whose Word they want to explain. The question is: when a religion is based on the "phenomenon of the Sacred Book," which has occupied our attention here as the principle and the source of spiritual hermeneutics, is it faithful to the spiritual sense when it wants to stop at itself and to stop the history of religions with itself, finding itself powerless to understand and validate any religious form that has come after it? For one does not "stop" history, inasmuch as one is situated in it and claims to "make history" oneself.

In Islam, Shi'ism defies simultaneously the past and the present through its eschatological expectation, by professing that after the conclusion of "law-giving prophecy," the religious future of humanity is not closed. Something is still to be expected, not only a "future" that gives its meaning to the "present," but an inrush of *metahistory* that makes evident the unidimensionality of our "historical consciousness." That inrush is signified by the advent of the Imām of the Resurrection, whom many Shi'ite authors expressly identify with the Paraclete, announced in the

Gospel of John (15:26, 16:13-14).[200] This eschatological expectation was an essential element in primitive Christianity. To the extent that in our time it has not become purely a matter of words, it alone can clarify the situation to which we are led inevitably, at one time or another, by comparative spiritual hermeneutics of the Bible and the Qur'ān, that is, hermeneutics of the "Sacred Book" as it is practiced, not by the literalists or rational dogmatists, since there is no result in that case, but by all those who are called mystics or mystic theosophers.

In other words, if not only a general theology of the *history* of religions but also a general theology *of religions* is necessary and conceivable, it cannot be established either as a synthesis or as a process of the "historical past." It is not feasible, in one form or another, except as a theology or a theosophy of the Paraclete. This begins when our bondage to the unidimensional and linear perspective of the consciousness called "historical" ceases. What we have called here *hierohistory* is the appearance of a *hieratic* dimension, heterogeneous to our historical time; the time of this hierohistory is the one that we have seen Swedenborg analyze as a succession of spiritual states, and the events that are visions—those of Isma'ili hierohistory, for example, or those that fill our cycle of the holy Grail—are *true* and *actually* take place "in that time."

I believe that for the first time, we have noted here certain hermeneutic convergences in a spiritual writer like Swedenborg, based on the Bible, and among the Isma'ili spiritual writers in Islam, based on the Qur'ān. We have only been able to indicate a very limited number of aspects, with regard to the hierohistory of Adam and that of Noah; there are a great many others to study. We would have to involve, from the Islamic side, all Shi'ite hermeneutics in general, all those of Sufism, those of Ibn 'Arabi, Semnānī, Ṣadrā Shīrāzī, etc. From Christianity, we would have to include all of Christian gnosis, the entire school of Jakob Boehme, and go as far as the extraordinary hermeneutic monument erected by Emil Bock. The task would be overwhelming.

Will it not impose itself upon us someday, though, in one form or another? We cannot yet foresee what may result, for example, from a comparison between the Christian theology of Swedenborg, who is neither trinitarian nor Pauline, with the specific form of Islamic Shiʿite theology, where imāmology assumes a function homologous to that of Christology in Christian theology.[201] But what one can foresee is that there is something in common between the idea of the *Nova Hierosolyma* and the *parousia* of the "Hidden Imām," identified with the Paraclete in the Twelve-Imām Shiʿite conception. Perhaps this foresight requires the spirit of spiritual freedom that we have heard signified in the order given to Noah: "Go forth from the Ark"—or in what Berdyaev called "Christ in motion," in contrast with the Christ of immutable dogma.

If the grand task of a general theology of religions was ever foreseen, it was surely by the great Protestant theologian of German romanticism, Schleiermacher, himself a master of hermeneutics. If he is scarcely to the taste or in the style of our time, this is perhaps owing to a symptom not only of dryness of heart in our theologies, but of resignation, of secret agnosticism, which insists that one should be more attentive to questions that are, in fact, at the level of sociology, even when they bear the name of ecumenism. In a striking page of his *Discourses on Religion*, a page totally inspired by the verses in John concerning the Paraclete, Schleiermacher professes that if, since the flowering of the first Christianity has passed, the Sacred Scriptures, the Bible, have come to be considered a closed code of religion, it is because it has been claimed that limits can be imposed on the boundless freedom of the Holy Spirit. In fact, it would be necessary to make it appear dead, and for that it would be necessary that religion itself—a divine work, not a human one—should be dead. Schleiermacher would not have spoken otherwise if he had been, like us, witness to the efforts of the theologians who have made themselves the accomplices of that death, by affirming, under the pretext of safeguarding the divine transcendence, that

Christianity is not a religion and by obstinately repeating that religion is only the work of man—as though man could be capable of this effort at salvation without God being its active Subject.

In contrast, Schleiermacher proclaims: "All those who have still felt their life in them, or have perceived it in others, have always declared themselves against that innovation which has nothing Christian in it. The Sacred Scriptures became the Bible by means of their own power; they do not forbid any other book to be or to become the Bible; they would willingly allow anything written with the same power to be added."[202]

This page of Schleiermacher could be the charter of all future comparative spiritual hermeneutics.

Notes

1. See below, note 150.

2. Regarding this theme, see our *Trilogie ismaélienne*, Bibliothèque Iranienne, vol. 9. (Paris: Adrien-Maisonneuve, 1961), pp. 137-144.

3. See *En Islam iranienne*, 3: 214 ff. and 4: index under *Gestalt*.

4. On the difference between the two, see our book *Avicenne et le Récit visionnaire*, Bibliothèque Iranienne, vol. 4 (Paris: Adrien-Maisonneuve, 1954), 1: 34 ff., and new ed. (Paris: Berg international, 1979), pp. 39 ff. Let the present study be the occasion to recall a memorable conversation with D.T. Suzuki here at Eranos, ten years ago (August 1954). The master of Zen Buddhism expressed the importance that he attached to Swedenborg and his work by the fact that, fifty years earlier, he had translated four of Swedenborg's books into Japanese. And he added: "He is your Buddha, for you Occidentals, it is he whom it is necessary to read and to follow!" Elsewhere, I have mentioned this conversation in greater detail (*Creative Imagination in the Sufism of Ibn 'Arabi* [Princeton: Princeton University Press, 1969], pp. 354-355, note 41).

5. The recent Swedenborgian bibliography includes the important works of Ernst Benz, *Emanuel Swedenborg, Naturforscher und Seher* (1948; Zurich: Swedenborg Verlag, 1969), and *Swedenborg in Deutschland* (Frankfurt am Main, 1947), as well as Friedemann Horn, *Schelling und Swedenborg* (Zurich: Swedenborg Verlag). Dr. Horn also publishes a journal of Swedenborgian studies, *Offene Tore, Beiträge zum neuen christlichen Zeitalter*, in which articles of great interest have been appearing since 1957.

6. Emanuel Swedenborg, *Arcana Coelestia*, trans. J. F. Potts (39th rpt.; New York: Swedenborg Foundation, 1984), §§ 241-243.

7. Ibid., § 2987.

8. Ibid., § 2988.
9. Ibid., § 2989, 2997.
10. Ibid., § 2990.
11. This is, for example, the fundamental doctrine professed by all the "eastern" theosophers (*Ishrāqīyūn*) of the school of Sohravardī in Iran, the doctrine called *al-imkān al-ashraf*, namely, that if a particular degree of being is given, this implies *eo ipso* the effective existence of the higher degree of being.
12. *Arcana Coelestia*, §§ 2991-2992.
13. Ibid., § 2994
14. It is a principle that is illustrated by many symbols in traditional literatures; see, for example, the theme of the "Green Island" among the Shi'ites, which provides subsistence to the "continent." *En Islam iranien*, 4: 390 ff.
15. *Arcana Coelestia*, §§ 2998-3000 (in the Ishrāqī lexicon: to see things in their *Malakūt*).
16. All this corresponds perfectly to what the *Ishrāqīyūn* describe as the "eighth climate"; see our book *Spiritual Body and Celestial Earth: From Mazdean Iran to Shi'ite Iran* (Princeton: Princeton University Press, 1977).
17. *Arcana Coelestia*, §§ 459, 684; Emanuel Swedenborg, *The True Christian Religion*, trans. John C. Ager (23rd rpt.; New York, Swedenborg Foundation, 1970), § 212; Emanuel Swedenborg, *Heaven and Its Wonders and Hell*, trans. John C. Ager (rpt.; New York: Swedenborg Foundation, 1960), the entire first part.
18. *Heaven and Hell*, §§ 191-195.
19. *Arcana Coelestia*, § 3223.
20. Ibid., §§ 3225-3226.
21. Ibid., § 3336.
22. Ibid., § 3337. Ṣadrā Shīrāzī's doctrine of the spiritual Imagination should be compared with this; see our article "La place de Mollā Ṣadrā Shīrāzī (ob. 1050/1640) dans la philosophie iranienne," *Studia Islamica* 18, (1963), summarized in *En Islam iranien*, 4: 54 ff.; as well as the texts translated in our book *Spiritual Body*.
23. *Arcana Coelestia*, § 3338.
24. Ibid., § 3340.
25. Ibid., § 3636.
26. Ibid., §§ 1116, 1118 ff.
27. Ibid., §§ 3342-3344.
28. *Heaven and Hell*, §§ 52 and 72. See our books *Cyclical Time and Ismaili Gnosis* (London: Kegan Paul International, 1983), pp. 113-114, and *Trilogie ismaélienne*, index under Temple de lumière. See infra the text preceding footnote 139.
29. *Arcana Coelestia*, § 2996. See also §§ 2988, 2989, 2997.
30. See index to the English translation of the *Arcana* published by The Swedenborg Society, London, p. 201, under *Esse*; and Emanuel Swedenborg, *Divine Love and Wisdom*, trans. John C. Ager (rpt. New York: Swedenborg Foundation, 1960), § 14.

31. *Arcana Coelestia*, § 4211.
32. Ibid., §§ 5310 and 9315 (and index to the English translation, p. 196).
33. See our work *Creative Imagination in the Sufism of Ibn 'Arabi*, pp. 124 ff. On the theme of theophanic metamorphoses, see "Epistula Apostolorum," chapter XIV, in M. R. James, *The Apocryphal New Testament*, p. 489, and our book *Cyclical Time*, pp. 59 ff.
34. *Arcana Coelestia*, § 10159.
35. Ibid., §§ 3636, 3643.
36. Ibid., §§ 49, 288, 477, 565, 1894, 8547.
37. Ibid., §§ 3637.
38. Ibid., no. 3633.
39. *True Christian Religion*, §§ 201-202.
40. Ibid., §§ 265 and 279. See Numbers 21:14-15, 27-30; Joshua 10:13; 2 Samuel 1:17-18. Swedenborg (ibid. § 279) was especially occupied with collecting the citations about these ancient Books. The "Book of the Wars of Jehovah" drew his attention as treating of the same victorious combat against the hells that was precisely the reason for the advent of the Lord in our world (ibid. § 265).
41. Ibid., § 202 (see also *Arcana*, § 10252).
42. *True Christian Religion*, § 266.
43. See the note by Dr. Friedemann Horn in his German translation of *True Christian Religion*, § 266, pp. 355 and 356.
44. *Arcana Coelestia*, § 66.
45. Ibid. A style that emerged from what had been held in such high esteem in the *Antiquissima Ecclesia*. This style, however, does not present a form that is continuous and of historical appearance, as does the "most ancient style"; it is discontinuous and practically never intelligible except according to the internal sense, where the most profound *arcana* are found; the latter form a perfect continuity, relating to the external man and the internal man, to the states of the *Ecclesia*, etc.
46. *Arcana Coelestia*, §§ 66 and 1409.
47. Ibid., §§ 1403-1404.
48. Ibid., § 66.
49. Ibid., §§ 1407-1408. Compare the Isma'ili interpretation of the "*ḥadīth* of the tomb": from the middle ground between literalist dogma and the tomb (the latter being philosophy), where it is necessary that dogmatic belief should die and be metamorphosed, the True Religion, which is *theosophia*, is restored to life. See my introduction to *Commentaire de la Qaṣīda ismaélienne d'Abū'l-Haytham Jorjānī*, Bibliothèque Iranienne, vol. 6 (Paris: Adrien-Maisonneuve, 1955), pp. 48 ff.
50. *Arcana Coelestia*, §§ 1409 and 1414.
51. Ibid., § 1405.
52. Ibid., § 64. Cf. no. 937.
53. Ibid., § 167.

54. Ibid., § 755:4.

55. See note 17.

56. *True Christian Religion*, § 210.

57. Ibid., § 212.

58. Ibid., § 214, and *En Islam iranien* 1:139 ff.

59. *True Christian Religion*, § 214: "From all this it is clear that the Word is the real Word in the sense of the letter, for inwardly in this there is spirit and life. This is what the Lord says: 'The words that I speak unto you, they are spirit and they are life (John 6:63).'"

60. *True Christian Religion*, §§ 207-208, and *Arcana Coelestia*, § 2899.

61. For what follows, see especially *Arcana Coelestia*, § 10355. In the prefatory matter to the recent French translation of *Heaven and Hell* (*Le Ciel, ses merveilles et l'Enfer, d'après ce qui a été vu et entendu* [Paris: 1960]), L.-J. Français formulates the idea of this succession in the following manner: "The order established by the Divinity is that there always exists on our earth a principal spiritual center, the possessor of a Revelation, and from this center spiritual light radiates more or less directly, more or less secretly, throughout the world. There have thus been four of these principal centers since the time of the first earthly humanity. They are Assemblies of men, guardians of the Revelation that has been given to them. In current terminology, the word that is appropriate for these assemblies is the word 'Church.' There have thus been four central or principal Churches until now." In the terminology adopted by L.-J. Français, these four successive central "Churches" are designated as the Adamic central Church, the Noachic central Church, the Israelitish Church, and the Christian Church. The Church of the New Jerusalem is the "fifth universal central Church." We are in agreement with the terminology, but we have the greatest reservations with regard to anything that could lead to confusion between the ideas of Swedenborg and those of a social reformer of the human community. As a corollary, we really do not see how television or spaceships can in any way awaken the secularized consciousness of our time to the feeling of the "spiritual," except, perhaps, through a preliminary renewal of analogical knowledge. We are still far from this, and for the moment the question is rather to prevent any possible ambiguity and confusion between the results of "advanced science," which relate to the physical, and what is correctly within the province of metaphysics. See *Le Ciel*, pp. 8-14.

62. *Arcana Coelestia*, §§ 920, 2896, 2995.

63. Ibid., §§ 1119-1121. "It has also been shown that the internal respiration of the men of the Most Ancient Church, which was from the navel toward the interior region of the breast, in the course of time, or in their posterity, was changed, and receded more toward the back region, and toward the abdomen, thus more outward and downward; and that at length, in the last posterity of that church, which existed immediately before the Flood, scarcely anything of internal respiration remained; and when at last there remained none of this in the breast, they were suffocated of their own accord; but that in some, external

respiration then began and, with it, articulate sound, or the language of spoken words. Thus with the men before the Flood the respiration was in accordance with the state of their love and faith; and at last, when there was no love and no faith, but a persuasion of falsity, internal respiration ceased; and with this, the immediate communication with angels, and perception." Ibid., § 1120.

64. Ibid., §§ 920 and 2897.

65. Ibid., §§ 920, 2899, 10355.

66. See *Offene Tore* no. 5 (1961):146 ff., the article by Robert Kehl, "Christentum oder Paulinismus?"; no. 2 (1962):53-60, "Christentum oder Paulinismus? Ein Briefwechsel zum obigen Thema"; no. 4 (1962):103 ff., R. Kehl, "Replik zu 'Christentum oder Paulinismus?'"

67. *Arcana Coelestia*, § 4060.

68. Ibid., § 10355, citing Daniel 2:43: "And whereas thou sawest iron mixed with miry clay, they shall mingle themselves with the seed of men; but they shall not cleave one to another, even as iron is not mixed with clay."

69. *Arcana Coelestia*, § 2118.

70. The commentary on chapters 28 ff. of Genesis in the *Arcana Coelestia* contains spiritual hermeneutics developed from Matthew 24:15 ff.

71. Compare the affirmation in Isma'ili gnosis to the effect that if it is possible to say that there was a time when the world did not exist and that there will be a time when it will no longer exist, this relates only to the transition from one period to another, from one cycle to another, but not at all to the totality of universes, constituting "eighteen thousand universes." See Nāṣīroddīn Ṭūsī, *Taṣawworāt*, ed. W. Ivanow (Leiden: Brill, 1950), p. 48 of the Persian text.

72. *Arcana Coelestia*, § 2117.

73. *True Christian Religion*, § 207.

74. *Heaven and Hell*, §§ 191-195. See *En Islam iranien* 4: index, under Nā-Kojā-Ābād; and the essay "*Mundus imaginalis* or the Imaginary and the Imaginal" in the present volume.

75. *Arcana Coelestia*, §§ 2-4.

76. Ibid., § 62.

77. Ibid., §§ 6-13.

78. Ibid., § 85.

79. Ibid., § 51.

80. Ibid., § 52.

81. Ibid., § 61.

82. Ibid., § 53.

83. Ibid., § 54.

84. Ibid., § 81.

85. Ibid., § 85, 88.

86. Ibid., § 95, 10284.

87. Ibid., § 74.

88. Ibid., § 97.

89. Ibid., § 82.

90. Compare this idea of sensitivity and spiritual senses with that in the work of Ṣadrā Shīrāzī (d. 1040/1650) (*ḥawāss rūhānīya*, spiritual sight, spiritual hearing, etc.); see *En Islam iranien* 1: 229 ff., 242 ff.; and our *Histoire de la philosophie islamique*, (Paris: Gallimard, 1964), 1: 83 ff.

91. *Arcana Coelestia*, §§ 104, 1383.

92. Ibid., § 1384.

93. Ibid., §§ 1385-1387.

94. Ibid., §§ 126-127.

95. Ibid., §§ 128-129.

96. Ibid., § 141. Cf. the work of the Swedenborgian theologian Alfred Acton, *An Introduction to the Word Explained* (Bryn Athyn: Academy of the New Church, 1927), pp. 149 ff.

97. *Arcana Coelestia*, § 139.

98. Ibid., §§ 147 and 150.

99. Ibid., §§ 148-149.

100. Ibid., §§ 150-153.

101. See sec. 4 (text preceding footnote 83).

102. *Arcana Coelestia*, §§ 54, 252, 476.

103. Ibid., § 105: "The 'tree of lives' is love and the faith thence derived; 'in the midst of the garden,' is in the will of the internal man. The will, which in the Word is called the 'heart,' is the primary possession of the Lord with man and angel. But as no one can do good of himself, the will or heart is not man's, although it is predicated of man; cupidity, which he calls will, is man's. Since then the will is the 'midst of the garden,' where the tree of lives is placed, and man has no will, but mere cupidity, the 'tree of lives' is the mercy of the Lord, from whom come all love and faith, consequently all life."

104. See *Heaven and Hell*, §§ 372 and 382.

105. *Arcana Coelestia*, no. 155.

106. This is the work entitled *Conjugial Love* (trans. Samuel M. Warren [rpt. New York: Swedenborg Foundation, 1954]) .

107. *Arcana Coelestia*, §§ 159 ff.

108. Ibid., § 194.

109. Ibid., § 196. With regard to *Geistleiblichkeit* (spiritual corporeality), see the pertinent statements of a Swedenborgian thinker, Chauncey Giles, in his book *The Nature of Spirit and of Man as a Spiritual Being* (London, 1883), p. 6: "Here is the point in which philosophers and Christians have made the mistake, fatal not only to all *true* knowledge, but to *all* knowledge of spirit. It has generally been assumed that the only way to arrive at a true idea of spirit, was to regard it as the opposite of matter in every respect. They reason in this way. Matter has form, therefore spirit has none. Matter has substance, therefore spirit has none. In this way they deny to spirit all possible modes of existence. The Christian stops here, and ends by simply affirming its existence, but denies that we can know anything more about it. But many push this destructive logic a step further, and deny the existence of spirit altogether. And this is the logical

result, for denial can never end in anything but negation and nothing. This is inevitable; and the Christian escapes this conclusion only by stopping before he reaches it. We must admit that there is a spiritual substance, and that this substance has form, or we must deny the existence of spirit altogether. No other conclusion is possible."

110. *Arcana Coelestia*, §§ 199, 202.

111. Ibid., §§ 200, 310. "Their state is therefore quite different from that of the antediluvians.... These are arcana with which the present generation are utterly unacquainted, for at the present day none know what the celestial man is nor even what the spiritual man is, and still less what is the quality of the human mind and life thence resulting, and the consequent state after death" § 310.

112. Ibid., §§ 208, 214, 218.

113. Ibid., § 306.

114. Ibid., §§ 307 ff., 310 ff.

115. Ibid., § 468. See § 460-467, which summarize chapter 5 of Genesis. "[460:] This chapter treats specifically of the propagation of the Most Ancient Church [the *Antiquissima Ecclesia*] through successive generations almost to the flood. [461:] The Most Ancient Church itself, which was celestial, is what is called 'Man (*homo*),' and a 'likeness of God' (verse 1). [462:] A second church which was not so celestial as the Most Ancient Church, is called 'Seth' (verses 2, 3). [463:] A third church was called 'Enosh' (verse 6); a fourth 'Kenan' (verse 9); a fifth 'Mahalalel' (verse 12); a sixth 'Jared' (verse 15); a seventh 'Enoch' (verse 18); and an eighth church 'Methuselah' (verse 21). [464:] The church called 'Enoch' is described as framing doctrine from what was revealed to and perceived by the Most Ancient Church, which doctrine, although of no use at that time, was preserved for the use of posterity. This is signified by its being said that 'Enoch was no more, because God took him' (verses 22, 23, 24). [465:] A ninth church was called 'Lamech' (verse 25). [466:] A tenth, the parent of three churches after the flood, was named 'Noah.' This church is to be called the Ancient Church (verses 28, 29). [467:] Lamech is described as retaining nothing of the perception that the Most Ancient Church enjoyed; and 'Noah' is described as a new church (verse 29)." For its part, Isma'ili gnosis knows perfectly well that the "age of Noah," for example, designates not his person but his period (see sec. 3 of part 2). The ten names enumerated above are also known to Shi'ite prophetology, with several alterations resulting from the Arabic writing system. See note 170.

116. We have already had occasion to mention above (sec. 3) the analogy of this conception to that of the *Qiyāmāt* in Isma'ili gnosis.

117. *Arcana Coelestia*, § 585.

118. See sec. 3.

119. *Arcana Coelestia*, § 597.

120. Ibid., § 605.

121. Ibid., §§ 599-604. See § 639: "That by the 'ark' is signified the man of that church, or the church called 'Noah,' is sufficiently evident from the de-

scription of it in the following verses [Gen. 5:14]; and from the fact that the Lord's Word everywhere involves spiritual and celestial things; that is, that the Word is spiritual and celestial. If the ark with its coating of pitch, its measurement, and its construction, and the flood also, signified nothing more than the letter expresses, there would be nothing at all spiritual and celestial in the account of it, but only something historical, which would be of no more use to the human race than any similar thing described by secular writers. But because the Word of the Lord everywhere in its bosom or interiors involves and contains spiritual and celestial things, it is very evident that by the ark and all the things said about the ark, are signified hidden things not yet revealed." Swedenborg remarks that the same is true in the case of Moses' cradle (Exod. 2:3) and the Ark of the Covenant. "In like manner the temple of Solomon was not holy at all of itself, or on account of the gold, silver, cedar, and stone in it, but on account of all the things which these represented." Isma'ili gnosis professes the same doctrine with regard to the esoteric (*bāṭin*) signified by the Ark and its structure.

122. *Arcana Coelestia*, § 605 and § 606: "The 'flood,' the 'ark,' and therefore the things described in connection with them, signify regeneration, and also the temptations that precede regeneration."

123. Ibid., § 609.

124. Ibid., §§ 301, 784.

125. Ibid., §§ 301-303, 784.

126. Ibid., §§ 607-608.

127. Ibid., § 790.

128. Ibid., §§ 660-662.

129. Ibid., §§ 705, 730.

130. Ibid., §§ 904-905.

131. Many *ḥadīth* of the Fifth and Sixth Imāms (Moḥammad Bāqir and Ja'far al-Ṣādiq) formulate, with some variations, the same fundamental idea. See Abū'l-Ḥasan Sharīf Nabaṭī Ispahānī, *Tafsīr Mirāt al-Anwār* (Teheran, A.H. 1375), p. 5. It is upon this same fundamental idea that the Shi'ite traditions base the necessity for the continued presence of the Imām in the world, even when it is a matter of his "concealed" presence, as it is for the Twelve-Imām Shi'ites; for it is by means of this presence of the one who knows and inspires the hermeneutics of the Book that the Book never dies and its sense always remains to come. See Kolaynī, *Kitāb al-Oṣūl mina'l-Kāfī, Kitāb al-Ḥojjat* (Treatise of the Imām), 10, 3rd *ḥadīth*. The commentary by Mollā Ṣadrā Shīrāzī is particularly dense on this point. See *Sharḥ al-Oṣūl* (lithogr.; Teheran, n.d.), p. 490.

132. For the entire second part of the present study, we will refer to our previously published research, esp.: *Trilogie ismaélienne*; *Histoire de la philosophie islamique*, part 1; *En Islam iranien*, 1: 219 ff.; Mollā Ṣadrā Shīrāzī, *Le Livre des pénétrations métaphysiques* (*Kitāb al-Mashā'ir*), Bibliothèque Iranienne, vol. 10 (Paris : Adrien-Maisonneuve, 1964).

133. See Nāṣir-e Khosraw, *Le Livre réunissant les deux sagesses* (*philosophie grecque et théosophie ismaélienne*), Bibliothèque Iranienne, vol. 3, (Paris: Adrien-Maisonneuve, 1953), p. 67 of our "Étude préliminaire."

134. Regarding this hierarchy, see *En Islam iranien*, 4:205 ff., 346 ff.

135. See the excellent summary by Sayyed Kāẓem Reshtī (d. 1259/1843) at the beginning of his commentary on the "Throne Verse" (*Sharḥ Āyat al-Korsī*) (Tabrīz, n.d)., pp. 1 ff., as well as his "Epistle on the Exoteric, the Esoteric, and Symbolic Exegesis" (*R. fī maqāmāt al-ẓāhir wa'l-bāṭin wa'l-ta'wīl*), in *Majmū'a* of 34 treatises (Tabrīz, 1276), pp. 366-368.

136. Semnānī even calculated the approximate number of volumes necessary! See *En Islam iranien*, 3: 226 ff.

137. That is why it is preferable to retain the name *Isma'ilis* to designate this branch of Shi'ism, and to reserve the name *Isma'ilites* as an ethnic designation that refers to an entirely different concept. Of course, the figure of Isma'il, son of Abraham, also plays a predominant role in Isma'ili prophetology; Isma'il was the titular Imām (*mostaqarr*) while Isaac was only the trustee Imām (*mostawda'*). After that, the real Imāmate entered into a sort of "secrecy" until the time when it reappeared, during the period of Muḥammad, in the line of Imāms descended from 'Alī ibn Abī-Ṭālib. In the interval, it was the "trustee" Imāms who occupied the "front of the stage" during each prophetic period, although the texts also inform us of the names of the real Imāms.

138. For the essential differences between the Isma'ilism of the Alamūt reform and the Isma'ilism of the Fatimid tradition, see esp. our two works *Trilogie ismaélienne* and *Histoire de la philosophie islamique*. See also our "Eighth Centenary of Alamūt," *Le Mercure de France*, February 1965.

139. See note 28, and our "Étude préliminaire" to the book by Nāṣir-e Khosraw, *Le livre réunissant les deux sagesses*, pp. 74, 81, 83 note 157, 87 ff., 91.

140. See the diagrams given in our book *Cyclical Time*, pp. 94, 96, and in *Trilogie ismaélienne*, p. 60.

141. See W. Ivanow, *Ismaili Literature: a Bibliographical Survey*, The Ismaili Society Series A, no. 15 (Teheran, 1963), pp. 32 ff. Qāżī No'mān (Abū Ḥanifā al-No'mān ibn Abī 'Abd-Allāh al-Tamīmī al-Qayrawānī, d. 363/974) was a prolific author, many of whose books have unfortunately been lost. He originally belonged to the Malikite rite, or, much more likely, was already a Twelve-Imām Shi'ite. As a young man, he entered the service of the Fatimid caliph al-Mahdī in 313/925. He is interesting in that he is recognized by both the Isma'ilis and the Twelve-Imām Shi'ites, that is, by the two great branches of Shi'ism. The book *Asās al-Ta'wīl*, to which we will refer particularly here, was translated into Persian by Mo'ayyad Shīrāzī (d. 470/1077), but the only manuscript known to date is a modern Persian translation (see W. Ivanow, *Ismaili Literature*, p. 47, no. 169). The present study is based in part on the edition of the *Asās al-Ta'wīl* issued by Aref Tamer in Beirut in 1960. Regrettably, this edition, collated from two unsatisfactory manuscripts, is itself defective and

incomplete; the alterations of the text have rendered certain passages incomprehensible, and the edition does not give precise qur'ānic references (numbers of suras and verses). We could not have completed our study if W. Ivanow had not kindly placed at our disposal, in Teheran, two other manuscripts of the work. We devoted an entire course to it at the École pratique des Hautes-Études (see the report in *Annuaire de la Section des Sciences religieuses* [1964-1965]: 89 ff.).

142. See *Histoire de la philosophie islamique*, 1: 118 ff., and *Trilogie ismaélienne*, first chapter of the second treatise, pp. 149 ff. of the French translation.

143. See *Trilogie ismaélienne*, chapters 31 and 32 of the *Livre des Sources* by Abū Ya'qūb Sejestānī, pp. 97 ff. of the translation. See also the end of sec. 4 of part 2 of the present essay.

144. In Twelve-Imām Shi'ism, the twelve letters symbolize the Twelve Imāms (themselves symbolizing with the twelve signs of the zodiac, the twelve streams that Moses caused to gush from the rock, the twelve leaders of the tribes of Israel, etc.). The structure is different, because the idea of the Imāmate is different and limited to Twelve Imāms. See *Trilogie ismaélienne*, index under "douze"; and Ṣadrā Shīrāzī, *Le Livre des pénétrations métaphysiques*, index under "Imām," "Quatorze Très-Purs," etc.

145. For this succession of cycles, see *Trilogie ismaélienne*, index under '"cycle," "*dā'irat*," etc. Qāżī No'mān does not discuss this in his *Asās al-Ta'wīl*; we are giving a brief overview here of the entire subject. See also *Cyclical Time*, pp. 78-84.

146. Regarding the esoteric sense of the *hexaēmeron*, see *Trilogie ismaélienne*, index under this term (other references given there as well). See also *Cyclical Time*, pp. 96-97, and my introduction to *Commentaire de la Qaṣīda ismaélienne*, pp. 74 ff. (on the "theosophy of history").

147. As was said above, Qāżī No'mān does not discuss the origin and succession of the cycles in his book, but for the *ta'wīl* there is not a word to be changed in the letter of the text, when the "prologue in Heaven" is understood as the Imām Honayd, father of "our" Adam, conversing with his *lawāḥiq*. The chapter about Adam in the *Kitāb Asās al-Ta'wīl*, pp. 50 ff. of the edition cited above (note 141), opens with a number of observations regarding the Imāmate and prophecy.

148. The qur'ānic references given in the original text of this article were according to the tradition of Koufa, generally followed in Iran; the numbering of verses corresponds to that in the old edition of the Qur'ān issued, in the West, by Flügel. For the convenience of readers, the present English translation of Corbin's article gives the numbering and translation found in *The Holy Qur'ān: Text, Translation, and Commentary*, by A. Yusuf Ali (Washington, D.C., 1946).

149. *Asās al-Ta'wīl*, pp. 54 ff.; *Cyclical Time*, p. 82; *Trilogie ismaélienne*, pp. 126 ff.

150. See references in the previous note. The initial origin of Iblīs-Satan

goes back to the "drama in Heaven," when the Spiritual Adam (*Adam rūḥānī*, celestial *Anthrōpos*, Angel of humanity), having wrenched from his own being the darkness that had immobilized him in doubt, cast it into the abyss, where it caused the appearance of our physical cosmos. During the cycles of epiphany, this form of Darkness (of dark fire) remained harmless and invisible. It reappeared as a terrible counterforce at the threshold of a cycle of occultation; more precisely, it is the agent of that cycle, for Iblīs had been with Adam as one of the Angels of the preceding cycle; antagonism thus breaks out. It is before the revelation of Iblīs's secret that the Angels, that is, the twelve *lawāḥiq*, understand that they themselves have crossed the boundary of transgression by asking: "Wilt Thou place therein [on earth]...?" For they wanted to say: "We did not think that God would create a being superior to us." They therefore sought refuge near the Throne (*'arsh*) and circumambulated it for a week. In relation to this subject, the *Asās al-Ta'wīl* (p. 57) recounts a very instructive *ḥadīth* regarding the origins of the temple of the *Ka'ba*. Imām Ja'far aṣ-Ṣādiq, while still a young man, was performing the rites of circumambulation in the company of his father (Moḥammad Bāqir, the Fifth Imām), when a mysterious stranger (a blond man dressed in two white robes) asked him about the origins of the temple. Imām al-Bāqir stated to him the episode that we have just read, and continued: "Descend to earth, said their Lord to the Angels, and build there a temple near which those of the children of Adam who will have committed a transgression will find refuge. They will circumambulate around the Temple as you yourselves have sought refuge near the Throne.... Thus, they built this Temple (the *Ka'ba*), but God removed it at the epoch of the Flood; it is now in the Fourth Heaven. And the Angels make the pilgrimage there until the day of the Resurrection. Afterward, Abraham built the present Temple on the foundations of the other." All this is of very dense signification for hierohistory. The Temple that is in the Fourth Heaven, the *Bayt al-Ma'mūr*, is the celestial archetype of the visible and earthly Temple of the *Ka'ba*, which is its *ḥikāyat* (imitation, "history"). Its origin is connected to a "drama in Heaven"; evil exists before earthly man, but is redeemed from that point on. The Flood is the epoch when the Temple built on earth by the Angels was finally removed to Heaven (as happened to the holy Grail); we have only the copy, the *ḥikāyat* (built on the *foundations* of the first Temple; now, the word *Asās*, "foundation," designates preeminently the Imām). Thus the esoteric sense of the history of Noah. Finally, regarding the "pilgrimage of the Angels until the day of the Resurrection," it should be recalled that the Isma'ili *da'wat* is the "potential paradise." By accomplishing the earthly pilgrimage to the *Ka'ba*, the Isma'ili initiate knows that, in doing so, his rite symbolizes with the pilgrimage of the Angels. Moreover, according to the tradition of Alamūt, it is earthly life that is itself the pilgrimage to the encounter with the "celestial Temple," of which the Imām is the foundation.

151. When the drama is transposed to its origin, in the person of *Adam rūḥānī*, third Angel of the pleroma who became tenth because of his error, it is

a matter here, too, of the "betrothed of the Spiritual Adam who returned to his paradise." See *Cyclical Time*, p. 179 note 58 (with other references).

152. Qāzī No'mān explains the literalist puerilities committed on this point, as well as on the subject of the "leaves of the garden" referred to farther on, by the influence of Jews converted to Islam, who were unfortunately not esoterists and who recounted what they believed they had read in the Torah (*Asās al-Ta'wīl*, p. 68). See also note 163.

153. Ibid., p. 59. The text states: man has twelve ribs on each side; those on the right side are the symbol of esoteric knowledge (*'ilm bāṭin*), those of the left side are the symbol of exoteric knowledge. The double lineage of Isma'ili prophetology (prophets and Imāms) therefore proceeds from a very different idea of the double prophetic lineage in Judeo-Christian prophetology. It is also necessary to recall here the twelve *Ḥojjat* of the day and the twelve *Ḥojjat* of the night. See *Trilogie ismaélienne*, index under the term.

154. For example, Nāṣir-e Khosraw, *The Book of the Two Wisdoms* (*Jāmi' al-Ḥikmatayn*), chap, 30, pp. 295 ff. of the Persian text. Regarding this "feminine" spiritual aspect of the Imāms, See our book, *Spiritual Body*.

155. *Asās al-Ta'wīl*, pp. 59 ff. "The garden (paradise) is the most sublime thing that God has created. God has made it good news [*boshrā, evangelion!*] for the faithful believers. He says: One day shalt thou see the believing men and the believing women—how their light runs forward before them and by their right hands: [Their greeting will be:] 'Good News for you this day! Gardens beneath which flow rivers! To dwell therein for aye! This is indeed the highest achievement'" (Qur'ān 57:12).

156. Regarding *apparentiae reales*, see *Spiritual Body*, index under this term.

157. *Asās al-Ta'wīl*, p. 60. The author makes a precise distinction between a natural symbol (the *ta'wīl* refers to the "intention" of the things themselves) and a parable (the *ta'wīl* refers to the intention of the writer). This is an essential distinction that the adversaries of symbolic exegesis do not always make.

158. See our *Histoire de la philosophie islamique* 1: 184 ff.; and our study "Le 'Livre du glorieux' de Jābir ibn Ḥayyān," *Eranos-Jahrbuch* 18 (1950).

159. This is the theme of one of the famous conversations between the First Imām and his disciple Komayl ibn Ziyād, the charter of "philosophy" for all Shi'ite thinkers. The text appears in the sixth part of *Nahj al-Balāgha*. The author presents only the first part of the conversation here. Regarding this, see *Trilogie ismaélienne*, index under "Komayl," and *En Islam iranien*, 1: 111 ff.

160. Compare this with the exegesis of Adam's transgression given in Twelve-Imām Shi'ism, for example, in Ḥaydar Āmolī's work: an act of madness, and perhaps sublime madness, because it was necessary that Adam depart from Paradise. See *En Islam iranien* 1: 97 ff.

161. *Asās al-Ta'wīl*, pp. 65-66.

162. It could also be said that the scission of the *ẓāhir* and the *bāṭin*, like the scission of the "masculine" and the "feminine," would correspond here to what Jakob Boehme symbolizes as the separation of Adam and the heavenly

Sophia, a reminiscence of which, at least, we have noted in Swedenborg.

163. *Asās al-Ta'wīl*, pp. 68-69. "This is a type of *ta'wīl* that is intolerable to the intellect, and that remains absolutely ineffective." See note 152. It does not seem that the Isma'ilis had much knowledge of Jewish gnosis, with which their own, however, has many affinities.

164. Ibid., pp. 66-67.

165. Ibid., p. 67. Regarding the "Words" that Adam learned from his Lord (Qur'ān 2:37), and that are the seven supreme Letters, the seven Cherubim, the seven Divine Words, see *Trilogie ismaélienne*, index under "sept"; and Ṣadrā Shīrāzī, *Le Livre des pénétrations métaphysiques*, index under "*Kalimāt tāmmāt*" (the Perfect Divine Words).

166. *Asās al-Ta'wīl, pp.* 69-70. Regarding the concept of *māddat*, see *Trilogie ismaélienne*, index under this term.

167. *Asās al-Ta'wīl*, p. 70. "The Messenger of God said: I receive the Divine Revelation (*waḥy*) from Gabriel; Gabriel receives it from Michael, and Michael receives it from Seraphiel; Seraphiel receives it from *Lawḥ maḥfūẓ* (*Tabula Secreta*, the Soul, the *Tālī*), which receives it from the *Qalam* (the Intelligence, the *Sābiq*). Thus, the *ta'yīd* (Divine Inspiration) is conjoined with the Enunciator-Prophets (*Noṭaqā'*) by the intermediary of five celestial dignitaries, and from the prophets it is conjoined with the *Mostajībūn* (the neophytes) by the intermediary of five earthly dignitaries." Regarding the archangelic pentarchy and the meaning of the designations *Jadd, Fatḥ, Khayāl* for the triad Gabriel, Michael, and Seraphiel, in the writings of Abū Ya'qūb Sejestānī and Nāṣir-e Khosraw, see our "Étude préliminaire" to Nāṣir-e Khosraw, *Le livre réunissant des deux sagesses*, pp. 91-112. For his part, Ja'far ibn Manṣūr al-Yaman (who wrote ca. 380/990) devotes many pages of his *Sarā'ir al-Noṭaqā'* to this theme (*Khayal* = Seraphiel, *Fatḥ* = Michael, *Jadd* = Gabriel. *Khayāl* assumes, in a way, the function of transcendental Imagination). See personal photocopy of a ms. of the *Sarā'ir*, fol. 7-9^{b}. Unfortunately, I cannot dwell on it here.

168. Regarding this theme, see a beautiful page by Nāṣir-e Khosraw: "Now the Earth is dark, and when the Resurrection comes, it will be an Earth of light.... That *other* Earth is now hidden in the night, until the light rises upon it. It is said of the other Earth that the esoteric sodality is founded upon it through firmness of faith—in spirit, and by no means in a material sense. That Earth is dark today, but it will become *Terra lucida*, and the darkness of the contradictory literalist exegeses will be dissipated by that splendor of light. It is upon the Book of God that our sodality is founded." See our "Étude préliminaire," p. 126.

169. It is the entire "drama in Heaven" causing the downgrading of the Third Angel to the rank of Tenth, our demiurge. See *Trilogie ismaélienne*, index under "Adam spirituel," "*ta'akhkhor*"; and Ṣadrā Shīrāzī, *Le Livre des pénétrations mystiques*, index under "*ta'akhkhor*."

170. *Asās al-Ta'wīl*, pp. 74-75. The importance accorded here to Seth (*Hibat Allah*, that is, Adeodatus, Nathanael) reminds one of the Sethian gnostics.

The names of the Imāms of the Adamic period are the names that appear in chapter 5 of Genesis: Seth, Enosh, Qinān (Kenan), Mahaliel (Mahālalel), Okhnokh (Enoch), Matūshalah, Lamek, father of Noah. See note 115. In the tradition of Alamūt, where the Imām takes precedence over the Enunciator-Prophet and is permanently *Mawlāna* (*Dominus noster*), the Imām of the periods of Adam, Noah, and Abraham is none other than Melchizedek.

171. *Asās al-Ta'wīl*, p. 87. The figure of 950 years corresponds to the one indicated in Gen. 9:28-29: "And Noah lived after the flood three hundred and fifty years. And all the days of Noah were nine hundred and fifty years; and he died." On the other hand, Qāẓī No'mān knows quite well that the age of the physical person of Noah did not exceed 125 years, which also agrees with Genesis 6:3: "for that he [man] also is flesh: yet his days shall be an hundred and twenty years."

172. Regarding the categories of prophets, see *En Islam iranien*.

173. *Asās al-Ta'wīl*, pp. 76-77. When speaking of him, Noah's enemies use the word *bashar* (man), which, in the current language, means the epidermis, the surface of the skin; they signify by this the *ẓahir* and use it to tell Noah that what he is bringing them they already know, and that he has no preeminence over them. The qur'ānic verses commented upon in their Isma'ili sense in the present section mostly come from sura 11 (Hōd) and sura 71 (Noah).

174. Ibid., p. 78.

175. The Imām of the Resurrection is often called the "seventh *Nāṭiq*," as though concluding the succession of the six great prophets (as the "seventh" day of the *hexaëmeron*), although he does not proclaim a new *sharī'at*, his role being to unveil the *ta'wīl*, the esoteric sense, of the revelations received by the preceding prophets. As the "seventh day," he is the perfect Man. It was seen that in Swedenborg's work, the "seventh day" is the celestial Man.

176. *Asas al-Ta'wīl*, pp. 79-80. Regarding the number twelve, see notes 144 and 153.

177. Ibid., pp. 81-82.

178. See ibid., p. 92, the commentary on the parallel qur'ānic verses (54:11 ff.): "*So we opened the gates of heaven, with water pouring forth, and We caused the earth to gush forth with springs.* The esoteric sense of the beginning of the verse is the opening of the *gates* [*bāb*] of the Enunciator, that is, of those whom Noah had appointed with a view to the exoteric of Knowledge, while the following part signifies the act of giving an outlet to gnosis from the dignitaries in charge of the esoteric, that is, the twelve *Noqabā'* appointed by Noah's Imām in each of the twelve regions [*jazīra*]. It is the same thing that is signified in the history of Moses by the twelve springs that Moses causes to gush from the rock by striking it with his staff (Qur'ān 2:60). *So the waters [from heaven] met [the waters that gushed forth from the earth] to the extent decreed*, that is, the science of the exoteric [that of the prophets] will meet the science of the esoteric [that of the Imāms and the *Noqabā'*], in the order that has been decreed or predetermined for them."

179. Regarding the co-responsibility of the *ḥodūd* until their *post mortem* becoming, see *Trilogie ismaélienne*, pp. 163 and 173 note 200.

180. See the diagrams to which we referred above, note 140.

181. *Asās al-Ta'wīl*, pp. 83-84.

182. Ibid., pp. 84-85.

183. Shem was the Imām appointed by Noah; see, however, what was stated in note 170, regarding Melchizedek.

184. *Asās al-Ta'wīl*, p. 86.

185. Ibid., p. 90.

186. Regarding this concept (*ta'akhkhor, takhallof*), see note 169.

187. *Asās al-Ta'wīl*, p. 89.

188. Ibid., p. 95, the beautiful final prayer of Noah (Qur'ān 71:28): "O my Lord! Forgive me, my parents, all who enter my house in faith, and all believing men and believing women" The "forgiveness" signifies reentry into the esoteric; the two parents are those who had received Noah into the *da'wat* and given him his spiritual education (that is, the last Imām of the period of Adam and his *Ḥojjat*); the believing men and believing women are all those men and women to whom, before him and after him, the *da'wat*, the *Ecclesia spiritualis universa*, was extended.

189. *Asās al-Ta'wīl*, p. 92.

190. Ibid., p. 86. Qāżī No'mān emphasizes the difference between the "departure from the Ark" and the "departure from Paradise." In fact, Adam was obliged to "descend" from Paradise for having wanted to attain to the *bāṭin* without the *ẓāhir* and doing violence to the knowledge of the Resurrection; in wanting to lay bare the *bāṭin*, it is his own nakedness (his darkness) that appears to him. Noah had received the order to "convoke" men to the *ẓāhir* and the *bāṭin*; but they refused, and the *ẓāhir* without the *bāṭin* (the huge waves) suffocated them. Noah receives the order to "descend" from the Ark when the "waters" (the esoteric) have withdrawn into the Imām.

191. *Asās al-Ta'wīl*, pp. 93-95 for this entire context. The Imāms of the period of Noah, like those of the period of Adam see note 170), bear names that appear in Genesis 10:10-27, albeit altered by the Arabic writing system: Arfakhshad (Arphaxad, son of Shem), Shālikh (Salah), 'Abir (Eber), Fālij (Peleg), Ra'ū (Reu), Sarūj (Serug), Tārikh (Terah, father of Abraham and his two brothers Nākhor and Haran). Ibid., p. 106.

192. See *'Oyūn Akhbār Imām Reżā* (Qomm, 1377), 1: 83-85. We will return to this elsewhere.

193. For all that follows, *Asās al-Ta'wīl*, pp. 291-313. We are giving an extremely abbreviated summary here.

194. This 'Imrān is carefully distinguished by our Isma'ili authors, as by many other commentators, from the 'Imrān of the family of Moses (see Qur'ān 3:33), just as the Aaron whose sister is Maryam here, is not the Aaron who is the brother of Moses, but a dignitary of the end of this period. There is homonymy, not an anachronism, which our authors would have been

prevented from committing, given their conception of each period of the cycle of prophecy.

195. For all that follows, the qur'ānic verses commented on are 3:35-36, 37-38, 45-47; 5:113, and sura 19 (Maryam).

196. The treatise entitled *Ghāyat al-Mawālīd*, attributed to Sayyid-nā al-Khaṭṭāb (d. 533/1138), after a long discussion as to whether a woman can be a *Ḥojjat*, responds in the affirmative. That was the case in Yemen, with the Princess al-Ḥorrat al-Malika. See W. Ivanow, *Ismaili Tradition Concerning the Rise of the Fatimids* (Oxford: Oxford University Press, 1942), p. 21.

197. Regarding Mary Magdalene (Maryam al-Majdalānīya), see *Cyclical Time*, p. 97.

198. Regarding the concept of *māddat*, see note 166.

199. *Asās al-Ta'wīl*, p. 313. See note 143.

200. See *Trilogie ismaélienne*, pp. 98-100 notes 196 to 202, and pp. 141 ff.

201. There are a number of texts by Swedenborg concerning Islam and Muslims, their "place in Heaven," etc., texts that are expressed either in terms of doctrine or *ex auditis et visis*. It would be important to group them together with a view to a special study of all the questions that are thus posed, especially the manner in which Swedenborg is in a position to value positively the prophetic message of Islam (*True Christian Religion*, § 833). Let us note, however, that where the expression "Son of God" appears as referring to "the wisest of prophets," it is appropriate to substitute the expression "Spirit of God" (*Rūḥ Allāh*), as it is customarily used in Islam to designate Jesus, son of Maryam.

202. Schleiermacher, *Discourses on Religion*, fifth discourse

Index